D1274294

Palgrave Macmillan's Digital Education and Learning

Much has been written during the first decade of the new millennium about the potential of digital technologies to produce a transformation of education. Digital technologies are portrayed as tools that will enhance learner collaboration and motivation and develop new multimodal literacy skills. Accompanying this has been the move from understanding literacy on the cognitive level to an appreciation of the sociocultural forces shaping learner development. Responding to these claims, the **Digital Education and Learning Series** explores the pedagogical potential and realities of digital technologies in a wide range of disciplinary contexts across the educational spectrum both in and outside of class. Focusing on local and global perspectives, the series responds to the shifting landscape of education, the way digital technologies are being used in different educational and cultural contexts, and examines the differences that lie behind the generalizations of the digital age. Incorporating cutting-edge volumes with theoretical perspectives and case studies (single-authored and edited collections), the series provides an accessible and valuable resource for academic researchers, teacher trainers, administrators and students interested in interdisciplinary studies of education and new and emerging technologies.

Series Editors:

Michael Thomas is Senior Lecturer at the University of Central Lancashire, UK, and Editor-in-Chief of the *International Journal of Virtual and Personal Learning Environments*.

James Paul Gee is Mary Lou Fulton Presidential Professor at Arizona State University, USA. His most recent book is *Policy Brief: Getting over the Slump: Innovation Strategies to Promote Children's Learning* (2008).

John Palfrey is Head of School at Phillips Academy, Andover, USA, and Senior Research Fellow at the Berkman Center for Internet & Society at Harvard. He is co-author of *Born Digital: Understanding the First Generation of Digital Natives* (2008).

Digital Education: Opportunities for Social Collaboration
Edited by Michael Thomas

Digital Media and Learner Identity: The New Curatorship
By John Potter

Rhetoric/Composition/Play through Video Games: Reshaping Theory and Practice of Writing
Edited by Richard Colby, Matthew S. S. Johnson, and
Rebekah Shultz Colby

Computer Games and Language Learning
By Mark Peterson

The Politics of Education and Technology: Conflicts, Controversies, and Connections
Edited by Neil Selwyn and Keri Facer

Digital Skills

Unlocking the Information Society

Jan A. G. M. van Dijk and
Alexander J. A. M. van Deursen

DIGITAL SKILLS
Copyright © Jan A. G. M. van Dijk and Alexander J. A. M. van Deursen, 2014.

All rights reserved.

First published in 2014 by
PALGRAVE MACMILLAN®
in the United States—a division of St. Martin's Press LLC,
175 Fifth Avenue, New York, NY 10010.

Where this book is distributed in the UK, Europe and the rest of the world,
this is by Palgrave Macmillan, a division of Macmillan Publishers Limited,
registered in England, company number 785998, of Houndmills,
Basingstoke, Hampshire RG21 6XS.

Palgrave Macmillan is the global academic imprint of the above companies
and has companies and representatives throughout the world.

Palgrave® and Macmillan® are registered trademarks in the United States,
the United Kingdom, Europe and other countries.

ISBN: 978–1–137–43702–0

Library of Congress Cataloging-in-Publication Data

Dijk, Jan van, 1952–
     Digital skills : unlocking the information society / by Jan A.G.M. van
Dijk and Alexander J. A. M. van Deursen.
         pages cm
     Includes bibliographical references and index.
     ISBN 978–1–137–43702–0 (hardback)
     1. Computer literacy. 2. Digital divide. I. Deursen, Alexander van.
     II. Title.

QA76.9.C64D544 2014
303.48'33—dc23   2014000950

A catalogue record of the book is available from the British Library.

Design by Newgen Knowledge Works (P) Ltd., Chennai, India.

First edition: July 2014

10 9 8 7 6 5 4 3 2 1

Contents

Illustrations

Boxes

Figures

Series Foreword

Much has been written during the first decade of the new millennium about the potential of digital technologies to radically transform education and learning. Typically such calls for change spring from the argument that traditional education no longer engages learners or teaches them the skills required for the twenty-first century. Digital technologies are often described as tools that will enhance collaboration and motivate learners to reengage with education and enable them to develop the new multimodal literacy skills required for today's knowledge economy. Using digital technologies is a creative experience in which learners actively engage with solving problems in authentic environments that underline their productive skills rather than merely passively consuming knowledge. Accompanying this argument has been the move from understanding literacy on the cognitive level to an appreciation of the sociocultural forces shaping learner development and the role communities play in supporting the acquisition of knowledge.

Emerging from this context the Digital Education and Learning series was founded to explore the pedagogical potential and realities of digital technologies in a wide range of disciplinary contexts across the educational spectrum around the world. Focusing on local and global perspectives, the series responds to the shifting demands and expectations of educational stakeholders, the ways new technologies are actually being used in different educational and cultural contexts, and examines the opportunities and challenges that lie behind the myths and rhetoric of digital age education. The series encourages the development of evidence-based research that is rooted in an understanding of the history of technology, as well as open to the potential of new innovation, and adopts critical perspectives on technological determinism as well as techno-skepticism.

While the potential for changing the way we learn in the digital age is significant, and new sources of information and forms of interaction have developed, many educational institutions and learning environments have changed little from those that existed over one hundred years ago. Whether in the form of smartphones, laptops, or tablets, digital technologies may be increasingly ubiquitous in a person's social life but marginal in their daily educational experience once they enter a classroom. Although many people increasingly invest more and more time on their favorite social media site, integrating these technologies into curricula or formal learning environments remains a significant challenge, if indeed it is a worthwhile aim in the first place. History tells us that change in educational contexts, if it happens at all in ways that were intended, is typically more "incremental" and rarely "revolutionary." Understanding the development of learning technologies in the context of a historically informed approach therefore is one of the core aspects of the series, as is the need to understand the increasing internationalization of education and the way learning technologies are culturally mediated. While the digital world appears to be increasingly "flat," significant challenges continue to exist, and the series will problematize terms that have sought to erase cultural, pedagogical, and theoretical differences rather than understand them. "Digital natives," "digital literacy," "digital divide," "digital media"—these and such mantras as "twenty-first-century learning"—are phrases that continue to be used in ways that require further clarification and critical engagement rather than unquestioning and uncritical acceptance.

The series aims to examine the complex discourse of digital technologies and to understand the implications for teaching, learning, and professional development. By mixing volumes with theoretical perspectives with case studies detailing actual teaching approaches, whether on or off campus, in face-to-face, fully online, or blended learning contexts, the series will examine the emergence of digital technologies from a range of new international and interdisciplinary perspectives. Incorporating original and innovative volumes with theoretical perspectives and case studies (single-authored and edited collections), the series aims to provide an accessible and valuable resource for academic researchers, teacher trainers, administrators, policymakers, and learners interested in cutting-edge research on new and emerging technologies in education.

Digital Skills: Unlocking the Information Society is a timely intervention in the debate about digital literacy and the digital media skills required by people living in today's information society. Preferring the broader term "digital skills" to the more popular "digital literacy" and "information literacy," the book discusses the significance of the social and psychological factors that influence user motivation vis-à-vis digital media. Indeed, digital skills better describe the types of interaction, performance, and communication required in addition to the knowledge implied by the term "digital literacy," to survive and develop in an information-rich society in which transactions take place immediately and in a variety of channels.

One of the book's main contributions is the way it identifies a framework of six key aspects under the general heading of "digital skills." These include operational skills (referring to technical competence), formal skills (such as those relating to browsing), information skills (related to searching, selecting, and evaluating information), communication skills (dealing with messaging, tweeting, and using various communication channels in online environments), content creation skills (referring to user-generated content, particularly in a Web 2.0 context), and strategic skills (content-related skills that allow people to use digital media for a particular goal).

Applying their historical understanding of the information society, the authors argue that today's web users require more than merely technical skills in order to function effectively. While interfaces have simplified interaction, additional skill sets are needed in order to truly take advantage of the opportunities presented by digital media. One of the most powerful aspects of the book is that it situates digital skills within a social context. Based on this positioning, education emerges as not the only way to improve digital skills; preventive measures and strategic policy choices can also contribute in meaningful ways to advancing developments in this field.

Digital Skills: Unlocking the Information Society is a clearly written and concise addition to the literature on the contemporary digital-divide and digital-literacy debates and makes important contributions to our understanding of the social context of these practices. It is acutely aware of the risks of allowing second-level digital divides (those focusing on skills gaps) to continue and in giving too much priority to the question of access to digital technologies. The book acts as a counter to this bias and highlights the consequences of allowing an "information elite" to develop at the expense of policies that aim to support diversity and equality of opportunity. Effective digital education and learning is still based on confronting these divides and while digital technologies have made content creation and generation easier than ever before, significant barriers continue to exist. The book will help practitioners, researchers, and policymakers to address the key questions and to develop a more finely grained analysis of this important debate.

Series Editors
Michael Thomas
James P. Gee
John G. Palfrey

Overview of the Book

The first chapter of this book defines digital skills as a crucial phase in the appropriation of digital technology. A framework of six digital skills is introduced: two medium-related skills consisting of operational skills (technical skills to command digital media) and formal skills (browsing and navigating, above all, on the web) and four content-related skills consisting of information skills (the ability to search, select, and evaluate information in digital media), communication skills (the ability to communicate on mostly the Internet), content creation skills (the ability to generate content), and strategic skills (using a digital medium as a means for a particular personal or professional goal). Such contemporary digital skills are just the latest media skills people have developed. Chapter 1 provides a snapshot of skills in history to show that an expanding and cumulative number of skills have appeared and that an ever larger section of the population requires these skills.

Chapter 2 describes the detailed framework of six digital skills when applied to the Internet. This framework is our main contribution to the field of digital literacy, competencies, skills, or whatever other term readers prefer. It addresses both scholars and practitioners. The framework is detailed and made operational so that it can be used in empirical research.

After making a firm basis of the digital skills subject and proposing a skills framework, in chapter 3 we discuss the social contexts of the use and skills of digital media, and whether digital skills are actually a problem for people and society. We will list a number of fields of participation in society (e.g., economy, politics, social, etc.) to describe the impact of digital skills. Then, the problem of a lack of digital skills can be better understood. Questions such as "Are unequal digital skills not simply a reflection of social inequality in general?," "Has the print media not shown the same inequalities, for example, unequal skills in reading and writing proficiency?," "Are the traditional media not unavailable anymore for every information and communication need?," and "Do people with a lack of digital skills not get sufficient support from others?" will be addressed.

After discussing the importance of digital skills, in chapter 4 the extent of the problem is estimated from empirical evidence. The proposed digital skills framework is applied in performance tests and surveys to determine digital skill levels of the population at large. What are the current levels of Internet skills of our framework among the population? All six types of skills will be carefully examined. Which social categories of the population show higher or lower levels of these skills?

Chapters 5 and 6 discuss the main solutions of the digital skills problem discussed in chapter 4. The main solutions are (1) improvement of technology design by making digital media more accessible or usable and (2) educational solutions. Chapter 5 is primarily addressed to designers and producers of technology. How can they help improve digital media? Is it possible to support users in intuitive ways so they do not have to learn much digital skills first? This would be the preventive solution. In chapter 6, the cure for less than perfect or unavoidable complex technology is offered: educational solutions of all kinds. This chapter will primarily appeal to teachers, coaches, and human resources officers and educational institutions. It will be argued that formal education, computer classes, and training are not the most frequently used ways to learn digital skills. The most frequently used ways are informal—learning by doing, trial and error, self-study, and asking for assistance. What are the advantages and disadvantages of formal and informal education in learning skills? What are the solutions currently practiced in regular schooling, adult education, and distance education? What educational tools and styles are offered for disadvantaged groups such as differently abled, illiterates, elderly, and migrant users?

The final chapter 7 summarizes the conclusions of the book and explores policy perspectives. Evidently, this chapter addresses not only the policy makers, but also the public opinion in general. Policy makers are governments, businesses, educational institutions, and organizations of consumers and digital media users such as support services and citizen initiatives. This chapter provides an overview of the currently available strategies and instruments for digital skills improvement, including the actors meant to use these instruments.

CHAPTER 1

Introduction

The Deepening Divide

In the first decade of the twenty-first century, the attention given to the so-called digital divide in developed countries gradually decreased. The common opinion among policy makers and the public at large was that the divide between those with access to computers, the Internet, and other digital media and those without access was closing. In some countries, 90 percent of households were connected to the Internet. Computers, mobile telephony, digital televisions, and many other digital media decreased in price daily while their capacity multiplied. On a massive scale, these media were introduced in all aspects of everyday life. Several applications appeared to be so easy to use that practically every individual with the ability to read and write could use them.

Yet, we posit that the digital divide is deepening. The divide of so-called physical access might be closing in certain respects; however, other digital divides have begun to grow. The digital divide as a whole is deepening because the divides of digital skills and unequal daily use of the digital media are increasing (Van Dijk, 2005). One can even claim that as higher stages of universal access to the digital media are reached, differences in skills and usage increase. In this book, we will argue that digital skills are the key to the entire process of the appropriation of these new technologies. These skills are vital for living, working, studying, and entertaining oneself in an information society.

We consider access to be the complete process of appropriation of a new technology. Having or possessing the required equipment and reaching a connection—obtaining so-called physical access—comprise only one step in this process. This step is a necessary one; however, it is not decisive in

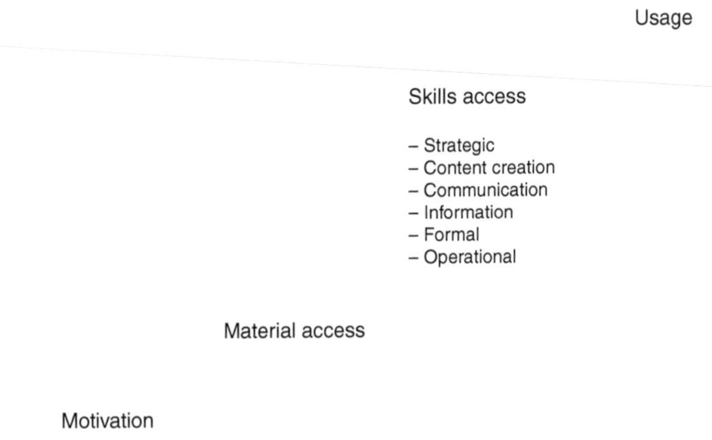

Usage

Skills access

– Strategic
– Content creation
– Communication
– Information
– Formal
– Operational

Material access

Motivation

Figure 1.1 Four Stages of Access to Digital Technology.
Source: Van Dijk, 2005, p. 22 (adapted).

the process that leads to the ultimate goal of satisfactorily utilizing the technology for a particular purpose. This can be explained using the model in figure 1.1.

Motivation is the first stage in the process of appropriation of a new technology. People who do not like computers or other digital media will not attempt to purchase one or obtain a particular connection, unless they are forced to do so. In the 1980s and 1990s, phenomena such as computer anxiety and technophobia were quite common. Fear of the new technologies touched a large part of the population, and negative or critical views of the effects of the new media on man and society were popular. In the second half of the 1990s, with the breakthrough of the World Wide Web and the increasing popularity of the Internet, these fears and views began to change. Around the year 2000, the Internet even turned into hype. In the decade that followed, the Internet merged completely into the everyday life of developed countries. At present, the elderly and people who are barely able to read and write are also motivated to obtain access to and use digital media, regardless of the perceived difficulty of these media. Instinctively, these people realize that they will become marginalized in society if they do not use digital media. However, computer anxiety still exists, and the levels of motivation differ substantially across sections of the population.

Motivation is not only crucial for the decision to purchase a computer and obtain a connection to the Internet but even more important for the steps needed to use these media and become familiar with them. Developing the necessary skills requires continuous effort and motivation. When all goes well, when the command and usage of digital media are simple, and occur according to the needs and goals of people, the result is stimulation. Then, a cycle of increasing motivation begins.

The second stage of appropriation, acquiring physical access to digital media, has completely dominated public opinion and policy perspectives in the last two decades. This dominance is evident in that many people believe that the access problem is solved and that the digital divide is closed when more than 90 percent of the population have a computer and Internet access. Then, the Internet can be put on par with television. Importantly, the diffusion of the Internet in the last two decades was even faster than that of television. While it took 17 years for television to reach a 30 percent household diffusion level in the United States, the Internet achieved the same rate in only 7 years (Katz & Rice, 2002). However, reaching the remaining population might be more difficult for the Internet than it was for television. In Northern and Western Europe and in South Korea, Internet access rates are reaching 90 percent figures; however, in Southern and Eastern Europe, they remain between 30 and 60 percent (Eurostat Statistics 2013). In the United States, household Internet access in 2012 was 81 percent, with large differences between urban and rural regions. However, on a world-scale, Internet access in 2012 was only 35 percent, with several developing countries below 10 percent (International Telecommunications Union, 2013).

Moreover, physical access is not equal to material access. Material access includes all costs of the use of computers, connections, peripheral equipment, software, and services. These costs are diverging in many ways, and people with physical access have quite different computer, Internet, and other digital media expenses. Differences in the types of connections and hardware employed, for example, have remained stable (e.g., Davison & Cotten, 2009; Pearce & Rice, 2013). Although the physical access divide will close in the long run, material access divides will remain and perhaps become even more prominent. The innovation of information and communication technologies (ICTs) is not slowing, and continually more or less expensive new hardware and software are invented. Service innovation also leads to greater or fewer expenses for those with different needs and incomes.

Access and Beyond

The third stage of the appropriation of digital media consists of the skills necessary to master them. The main message of this book is that these skills are the key to the entire process. We prefer to use the term "skills" over "literacy" or "competence," which are concepts that are also frequently used in the literature (separately or in combinations such as "literacy skills" or "literacy competence"). Literacy can be considered the most general concept and is often considered as a set of skills or competencies. The term "literacy" has had a variety of meanings over time. The simplest form of literacy involves the ability to use language in its written form: "A literate person is able to read, write, and understand his or her native language and express a simple thought in writing" (Bawden, 2001, p. 220). A more general definition considers literacy as the skills that are needed to perform well within society. When the context is also considered, being literate becomes "having mastery over the process by means of which culturally significant information is coded" (De Castell & Luke, 1988, p. 159).

Anttiroiko, Lintilä, and Savolainen (2001) concluded that there are two dimensions of competence: knowledge and skills. They defined knowledge as the understanding of how our everyday world is constituted and works, whereas skills involve the ability to pragmatically apply, consciously or unconsciously, our knowledge in practical settings.

In our view, the term "skills" suggests a more (inter)active performance in media use than, for example, the term "literacy," which refers to reading and writing texts. For instance, using the Internet extends beyond reading and writing on keyboards and screens to include interacting with programs and other people, or completing transactions for goods and services. Internet use requires more action than the relatively passive use of visual media such as television or books, which mainly require knowledge and cognitive skills. Thus, in addition to tool-related skills, specific skills are also needed to use the provided information or communicate over the Internet. The following chapters will extensively discuss different types of digital skills. We propose the following skills: operational, formal, information, communication, content creation, and strategic skills. These skills are overviewed at the end of this section and fully explained in the following chapter. They are the central part of this book.

The fourth and final stage of appropriation of digital media reaches its ultimate destination, usage. Usage is determined by two large factors: motivation (interest in particular applications and in the use of computers and the Internet in general) and skills (Van Dijk, 2005). Usage patterns consist of the frequency and length of time per day that the digital medium is used, the number and variety of applications, the types of applications used (for example, information, communication, commerce, work, entertainment, and education), and the type of use (productive and user-generated or consumptive). All of these variations are correlated with the demographics that are frequently examined in digital-divide research, that is, age, gender, educational level, occupation, household composition, and ethnicity (e.g., Hargittai & Hinnant, 2008; Livingstone & Helsper 2007; Van Deursen & Van Dijk, 2014a).

In this book, we will show that usage is also correlated with one or more of the skills mentioned in the former paragraph, although not in the simple and straightforward way that many suppose. It is common opinion that skills are developed with increasing frequency and time of use or what is called experience. We will show that this applies partly to the operational and formal skills, but not to the "higher" content-related skills of information, communication, content creation, and strategy. These are social and intellectual skills that must be developed before one begins to use computers, the Internet, and other digital media. While using digital media, these skills must be transformed and adapted to the special information, communication, and strategic requirements of the medium concerned. For example, searching for information in a library is quite different from searching for the same information in a search engine on the Internet.

With the large-scale diffusion of digital media in society and everyday life, many variations in the use of these media tend to grow as they mix with social, economic, and cultural differentiations in society. As these differentiations have also grown in contemporary (post)modern society, social and usage differences are likely to reinforce each other. The same is true for skills and for social, economic, and cultural differences. In this book, we will show that the skill levels attained differ among social and demographic categories. In addition, these skill differences create greater or fewer opportunities in social positions, for example, in the employment market and social networking.

With further diffusion of the digital media into society, the focus of the digital divide extends beyond physical or material access and shifts to the stages of skills and usage. In the digital-divide literature after the year 2000, this is expressed with different, but similar, concepts. Kling (2000) suggested a distinction between technical access (material availability) and social access (the professional knowledge and technical skills necessary to benefit from information technologies). Attewell (2001) has distinguished between first and second digital divides. Hargittai (2002) suggested the most familiar expression of a first- and second-level digital divide. DiMaggio and Hargittai (2001) suggested the following five dimensions along which divides may exist: technical means (software, hardware, and connectivity quality), the autonomy of use (location of access and freedom to use the medium for one's preferred activities), use patterns (types of uses of the Internet), social support networks (availability of assistance with use and the size of networks to encourage use), and skill (one's ability to use the medium effectively). Warschauer (2003) argued that besides physical access, factors such as content, language, literacy, educational level attained, and institutional structure must be considered. Van Dijk (2005) has made the four-stage distinction that is shown in figure 1.1.

Among all of these concepts and types of access to the digital media and beyond, this book will concentrate on skills. In our opinion, skills are increasingly the key variable of the entire process of access and information inequality in the information society.

A Range of Skills

In this book, we propose the following range of skills:

1. *Operational skills*. The popular and policy attention to digital skills is completely focused on "operational skills." These are the technical competencies required to command a computer or the Internet. In popular language, they are called "button knowledge."
2. *Formal skills*. In the improved interpretations of these technical competencies, attention is paid to browsing and navigating the Internet. This is what we call "formal skills." Every medium requires such skills because each has a number of formal characteristics. A book has chapters, paragraphs, a table of contents, and sometimes an index and references. Television has channels and programs. The Internet has sites with menus and (hyper)links. Users must learn these characteristics with every medium. Computers and the Internet are no exception. It is known that many elderly and illiterate people have problems thinking and acting in terms of menu structures and using hyperlinks.
3. *Information skills*. Less attention has been paid to so-called information skills, the ability to search, select, and evaluate information in digital media. These are especially needed in media that offer an overload of sources and content to choose from, such as the Internet. While operational and formal skills are medium-related skills, information skills are content-related.
4. *Communication skills*. "Communication skills" are needed for digital media such as the Internet that increasingly concentrate on communication. The use of email, chatting, instant messaging or tweeting, preparing profiles on social media or online dating, and contributing to online communities require special communication skills; however, there is no school to learn them.
5. *Content creation skills*. In the last ten years, "content creation skills" have become increasingly important, as the Internet has developed

from a relatively passive content consumption medium to a medium that enables actively produced user-generated content. This development is known as Web 2.0. Content creation is no longer only the design and publication of a personal or professional website, as in the 1990s; it also refers to the writing of text (as in blogs, Tweets, or on online forums), the recording or assembling of pictures, videos, and audio programs (as in photo, video, or music exchange sites), or compiling a personal profile and producing messages and images on a social networking site. These activities previously required professional skills. However, accessible software on the web now seems to offer nearly every individual the opportunity to develop amateur skills for these activities. The software is often deceivingly simple, leading the users to believe that they can make effective contributions to the web. In this book, we will argue that effective user-generated content on the Internet requires digital skills that must be learned.

6. *Strategic skills*. These skills refer to the ability to use the digital medium as a means for a particular personal or professional goal. For instance, while using one of the many applications of the Internet, one must make choices continually. Examples include comparing prices in ecommerce or making a reservation for the cheapest and most convenient flight. Strategic skills are also content-related skills. Regarding the Internet, these strategic skills could be called higher Internet skills together with information and communication skills. Lower Internet skills are "simply" browsing and navigating and operating Internet software.

The range of six types of skills is best characterized by the distinction between medium-related skills and content-related skills. The medium-related skills account for the technicalities of media use, apparent in the operational and formal skills, whereas the content-related skills account for the aspects that relate to the content provided by the media, apparent in the information, communication, content creation, and strategic skills. The distinction has a sequential and conditional nature. In other words, the skills come after and on top of each other. For example, performing content-related skills requires the command of medium-related skills, and strategic skills will not be effective without control of information and communication skills.

In the discussion of skills in this book, we will focus on Internet skills for two basic reasons. First, the Internet has become the most dominant digital medium that is linked to all other digital media. Gradually, personal computers have become terminals for Internet use. Digital televisions, telephones, cameras, and videos are increasingly connected to the Internet for transmission, reception, and exchange of user-generated content. A second, and even more important, reason is that in the context of Internet use, we are able to observe the entire spectrum of the proposed digital skills. However, at the end of this chapter, we will also elaborate on skills for traditional media.

A Snapshot of Skill History

The history of media skills that people require to function in society is marked by the following three epochal tendencies:

- An expanding and cumulative number of skills;
- Ever-larger sections of the population that require these skills;
- Education of these skills that shifts from private to public settings.

We will briefly describe these tendencies in a snapshot historical overview.

Until fairly recently, that is, the second half of the nineteenth century, societies were predominantly oral cultures. The majority of the population was not able to read and write. Individuals did not require these skills because work was manual and the entire day was needed to earn a living. After the invention of writing approximately five thousand years ago, reading and writing remained specialized activities for a small, elite of religious ministers, scholars, and rulers. The remaining population did not feel disadvantaged or harmed by their lack of reading and writing skills.

People in the European Middle Ages also primarily lived in an oral culture that was characterized by obedience to the church and working for survival. The limited schooling available was controlled by the church and mainly focused on reciting religious texts and performing church duties. Although most people became increasingly aware of the existence and significance of written documents, likely no more than 10 percent of the general public in Europe could read or write until approximately 1500 (Mizrach, 1998). The invention of the Gutenberg printing press in 1439 brought the printed book, which required new formal skills of reading and writing books (such as working with chapters and paragraphs, tables of contents, indexes, and references), but these were relatively minor additional skills.

Even between the seventeenth and the end of the nineteenth century, most people lacked reading and writing skills, as the vast majority of the population was needed for manual work in agricultural and industrial production. However, around the seventeenth century, with the increasing demands of trade, traffic, small industries, and state apparatuses, the demands for schooling increased, resulting in more people with the ability to read and write. Schooling, however, remained restricted to the higher classes of society. In the eighteenth century, most men were convinced that the education of the poor would be dangerous because it would encourage them to aspire beyond their status and to threaten social stability and the domination of the elite (Stone, 1969).

At the end of the eighteenth century, the Enlightenment appeared. This inspired Thomas Jefferson to propose his "Systematic Plan of General Education" in 1779. Shortly afterward, the first state-supervised schools appeared in the United States and Europe. These schools expanded the reach of formal education, and a greater number of people attended schools for longer periods of time (Rury, 2005). This was a historic step because until that time, schooling was a privately organized affair in particular churches and the domestic settings of guilds and small crafts in agriculture and industry.

After the industrial revolution and the expansion of urbanization, the skills of reading and writing became increasingly important due to the increasing complexity of production, distribution, circulation, and consumption systems (Beniger, 1986). During this time, the foundation was made for the contemporary information society. The organization of schooling by society was further strengthened by the introduction of compulsory education throughout the second half of the nineteenth century in most developed countries. This was another historic step. For the first time in history, the command of reading, writing, and other knowledge-based activities became obligatory for the entire population. From this time forward, it became increasingly difficult to maintain oneself in society without these literacies. In United Nation's Declaration on the Rights of the Child of 1959, this was acknowledged on a global scale. The declaration stated that children should receive compulsory education, at least in the elementary stages.

In the course of history, new technological innovations arose that required new skills. We previously mentioned the advent of the printing press and the book. In the communication revolution at the turn of the twentieth century, which was a response to the control revolution in the organization of society after the industrial revolution (Beniger, 1986), a host of new media appeared. In addition to new telecommunication media, the new media ranged from photography and film to the gramophone, radio, and television. The most important common denominator of these media is their audiovisual nature. Audiovisual media required new skills on top of the skills of reading and writing texts. However, these skills were barely a part of schooling. Similarly, the use of the new telecommunication media was not learned at school. The popular view prevailed that every individual is able to speak, hear, and view. Thus, learning to use audiovisual media was considered to be a hobby or a matter of professional expertise for a few.

This was not the prevailing popular view with the advent of the personal computer in the 1970s. On the contrary, this medium was conceived to be difficult and to require a number of advanced new skills. In terms of the six skills explained above, the main skills were considered to be the operational skills of commanding computer hardware and software. When the Internet arrived, it was first conceived as a type of computer medium that required the same operational skills and some additional skills for networking. Later, the Internet was transformed into the World Wide Web. Many people thought that its graphical interfaces with pictures, sounds, and videos were so accessible that even the barely literate could use it by simply clicking on icons.

In contrast, we claim that the Internet requires not less, but more skills than traditional media and computers. The skills defined in this chapter have a sequential and conditional nature. Computer users should be able to not only calculate but also read and write. Multimedia users require some understanding of audiovisuals. Internet users must be able to operate a computer. The same is true for tablets and small notebook computers, although touchscreens and icons simplify the operations. Without the skills of reading and writing and without understanding graphics or audiovisuals, people can barely use these media. To fully benefit from the opportunities of the Internet, users must command a long list of skills developed in the context of both traditional and digital media.

A First Inventory of Traditional and Digital Skills

We briefly described the list of skills elaborated in this book, namely, operational, formal, information, communication, content creation, and strategic skills. Before fully exploring these skills for the Internet in the next chapter, we make an inventory of these skills as applied to the most important media, namely, print, audiovisual, computer, and Internet media. This inventory will demonstrate that these media require comparable operational, formal, information, communication, content creation, and strategic skills. By proposing this inventory, an initial general definition for all of these skill types is proposed. In boxes 1.1 and 1.2, we summarize a comparison of traditional (print and audiovisual) and digital media (computer and Internet). We compare them with medium-related skills (operational and formal) and content-related skills (information, communication, content creation, and strategic). Medium-related

Box 1.1 Medium-Related Skills for Traditional and Digital Media

	Print media	Audiovisual media	Computers	Internet
Operation skills	Read and write texts and figures.	Read and write texts and figures; Watch, listen, record, and edit audiovisuals, possibly guided by text or icons.	Read and write texts and figures; Watch, listen, record, and edit audiovisuals, possibly guided by text or icons; Operate hardware; Operate software.	Read and write texts and figures; Watch, listen, record, and edit audiovisuals, possibly guided by text or icons; Recognize and operate the Internet service's toolbars, buttons, and menus; Use different types of user input fields found in Internet services; Manage different file formats in Internet services.
Formal skills	Understand and possibly edit the structures of texts: Chapters, paragraphs, references, index, and table of contents.	Understand and possibly edit the structures of audiovisuals: Scenes, shots, sequences, scenarios, starts, and endings	Understand and possibly edit the structures of computers: Drives, folders, and files; Keep a sense of orientation working with folders and files.	Understand and navigate hypermedia structures; Maintaining a sense of location while navigating on the Internet.

Box 1.2 Content-Related Skills for Traditional and Digital Media

	Print media	Audiovisual media	Computers	Internet
Information skills	Search, select, process, and evaluate information from printed text and figures	Search, select, process, and evaluate information from text, figures, video, images, and sounds.	Search, select, process, and evaluate information from text, figures, video, images, and sounds in computer software.	Search, select, process, and evaluate information from online text, figures, video, images, and sounds.
Communication skills	Encode and decode messages in order to construct, understand, and exchange meaning in text and figures.	Encode and decode messages in order to construct, understand, and exchange meaning in audiovisuals possibly guided by text or icons.	To encode and decode messages in order to construct, understand, and exchange meaning interacting with computer interfaces and software.	To encode and decode messages in order to construct, understand, and exchange meaning in interactive applications of the Internet.
Content-creation skills	Create texts of a specific kind requiring a particular plan or design: A letter, an article, a book, a review, etc.	Create audiovisuals of a specific kind requiring a particular plan or design: a sound recording, a video, a movie, etc.	Create a computer program or software of a specific kind requiring a particular plan or design: a new computer program or one adapted: a template, macro, frame, profile, etc.	Create contributions to the Internet of a specific kind requiring a particular plan or design: a personal website, a blog, a posting to a forum or online newspaper, an own video, a personal profile, etc.
Strategic skills	Orient, decide, and act upon information in printed texts and figures to reach a particular goal and eventually derive benefits.	Orient, decide, and act upon audiovisual information to reach a particular goal and eventually derive benefits.	Orient, decide, and act upon information in computers to reach a particular goal and eventually derive benefits.	Orient, decide, and act upon information retrieved online to reach a particular goal and eventually derive benefits.

skills refer to the technical aspects that are related to the use of the medium, whereas content-related skills address the substances provided by the medium.

The common denominator of operational skills is that the use of all media requires certain technical abilities to perceive and process the signs and symbols concerned and to command the particular hardware and software. All media have particular formal structures that users should learn. Subsequently, all media offer particular contents that enable users to search, select, process, and evaluate information. The media can also be used for communication, which encompasses encoding and decoding messages to construct, understand, and exchange meaning. All media can be used for content creation, from writing a book and making audiovisual programs to software programming and publishing a website, blog, web-video, or personal profile on a social networking site. Finally, all media can be approached with strategic skills as a means to reach particular benefits or goals.

Operating skills needed for *print media* are the skills of reading and writing texts and figures illustrating texts. Formal skills of using print media are the skills to understand and possibly edit the structures of texts. Every early reader of texts needs to recognize the forms of chapters, paragraphs, footnotes, references, indexes and tables of contents. Information skills for using a print medium are the skills required to search information, select relevant information, process the information, and evaluate the information found. Applying information skills in print media can be difficult because such media are mainly text-based and therefore require substantial mental effort to extract narrative meaning (Salomon, 1977; Newhagen & Bucy, 2004).

Communication skills in print media refer to the use and production of text in print form in order to encode or decode, or to produce and consume meaning that is exchanged between people. The form can be a letter, a memo, an article, a book, or whatever.

Content creation skill is the ability to produce these forms of printed texts with an ability to create the spelling, style, and page design that belong to the particular form. Content creation skills make a person a competent letter writer, author, journalist, or any other print content creator.

Strategic skills relate to the purpose of using the print medium and the potential empowerment that this usage provides. The purpose might be knowledge, message exchange, or entertainment. From the information obtained, a user might take actions, make decisions by placing this information in the correct perspective, and gain certain benefits that affect his/her personal or professional life. Entertainment might also be a goal among these purposes; the goal or the means do not have to be "information" in a narrow sense.

Audiovisual media, such as radio and television programs, movie pictures, and videos, originally mainly provided sounds, video, or images that could largely be processed without print media skills (Reeves & Nass, 1996). After some time, audiovisual media increasingly became filled with text in introductions, subtitles, text boxes, and banners. In addition to reading and writing, operational skills for using audiovisual media encompass attentive and systematic watching, listening, recording, and possibly producing and editing audiovisuals. The formal skills needed for audiovisual media include the understanding and possibly editing of the structures of audiovisuals, such as scenes, shots, sequences, scenarios, starts, and endings.

Information and strategic skills for the content provided by the audiovisual media require different mental operations than processing texts, for example, processing images and sounds. However, the set of actions required—searching, selecting, processing, and evaluating information—can be described using the same concepts. However, communication skills are rather different for audiovisual media. Encoding, decoding, and exchanging meaning with images and sounds require the capacity to know and use the effects of visuals, sounds, speech, and body language. Regarding strategic skills, it is relevant to know which audiovisual information can be used for taking actions and for making decisions. For example, the actions required differ for the goal of information retrieval and the goal of entertainment (Salomon, 1977).

In both print and audiovisual media, knowledge can be derived. The characteristics of traditional media (e.g., low levels of selectivity and accuracy of information compared to digital media) stimulate a relatively passive manner of media use, despite all justified claims of the so-called active audience. While traditional media *enable* active mental processing, digital media *require* a minimum level of active engagement with the medium and offer the possibility of interactions, transactions, and interpersonal communication. This is further explained below.

The primary operational skills for using *computers* are similar to those of print and audiovisual media. The skills of reading and writing texts and figures and watching, listening to, recording, and editing audiovisuals must also be used to operate computers. However, additional skills are required for the operation of computer hardware and software. The formal skills for using computers are new because they address a structure that differs from any other traditional medium, for example, using drives, folders, and files. This structure must be understood and mastered before effective use is possible. One not only needs to know how to open folders or save files, but also must maintain a sense of orientation while browsing through the numerous files and folders that hard drives often contain.

The content-related skills for using computers—information, communication, content creation, and strategic skills—are similar to the equivalent skills in traditional media. In using computers, information skills such as searching, selecting, processing, and evaluating information from integrated digital texts, images, sounds, videos, and figures are needed. Communication skills for computers are encoding and decoding messages to construct, understand, and exchange meaning while interacting with computer interfaces and software. Content creation for computers refers to creating a computer program or software of a specific type that requires a particular plan or design, for example, a new computer program or one adapted in the shape of a template, macro, frame, profile among others. Finally, strategic skills are the orientation, action, and decision required for processing this information to reach a particular goal and eventually gain a personal or professional benefit.

Similar to computers and audiovisual media, *the Internet* provides both verbal and nonverbal meaning and the need to manage both. The operation of an Internet browser is added to operational skills. Formal Internet skills require a unique form of digital skills for the adequate use of a browser and hypermedia. In hypermedia, users can choose their own nonlinear paths, providing substantial user control. They can move forward, backward, and to unknown locations. Without a sense of location, distance, and direction, users often experience a strong sense of disorientation (Kwan, 2001).

The information skills required for traditional media and computers are somewhat similar to those needed for the Internet. The difference is that the information provided by the Internet is infinitive, placing much more pressure on content-related skills. When, for example, a broad search strategy is used in an Internet search engine, a large amount of unsuitable results will appear, making selection one of the information skills that is more difficult to achieve. Information skills are involved when people want to reach a particular goal on their own initiative following a particular explicit question. Subsequently, the sources found should be evaluated for validity and reliability.

Compared to information skills, online communication skills are rather different from those of other media. One must learn to communicate in online or virtual environments with the reduction of nonverbal behavior cues. One must also become accustomed to patterns of asynchronous communication and a flood of messages that are unknown in many traditional media. It is not surprising that people must learn effective emailing, instant messaging, online profiling, online debating, and many other communication applications of the Internet.

On the same level as information and communication skills, other skills are (ever more) important needs for new applications on the Internet. The areas of entertainment and transaction have become increasingly popular on the Internet. Several entertainment skills for the Internet are easily distinguished, such as the skills to play online games and to act in virtual worlds.

The same is true for the transaction skills needed for online auctions, trade in online stocks or bonds, and other financial services. In this book, we focus on the current two most important applications, information retrieval and communication.

The fifth type of Internet skills is content creation skills. In the context of the rise of Web 2.0, these skills are increasingly important for Internet users. These skills are needed to create contributions to the Internet of a specific type that requires a particular plan or design, for example, a personal website, a blog, a posting to a forum or online newspaper, a home video uploaded to YouTube, and a personal profile in a social networking site.

The sixth type of Internet skills, strategic skills, assumes additional analytic abilities. Beyond the analysis of information sources, distinctions must be made between goals and means and between what is more and less important to reach these goals; finally, decisions should be made for a particular action. Thus, to acquire strategic skills and employ them on the Internet, users must be critical, analytical, and have a high degree of information skills.

Digital Skills: What Is New

In the past four years, we have made several empirical observations of the level of digital skills among cross-sections of the Dutch population using performance tests conducted in our laboratory. The results of these observations are a large part of the input for this book. After publicizing the results of these observations, which highlighted the large inequalities of digital skills among the people observed, we received many replies questioning the importance of this observation. Haven't all media, both old and new, been used with unequal skill by, for instance, those with high and low education? What is new about this?

As discussed, traditional and digital media skills contain many similarities. However, we claim that digital media skills increase the differences observed in traditional media skills. On the one hand, computers and the Internet make things easier because they enable systematic information retrieval from innumerable sources simultaneously. Finding information in a traditional library might be more difficult for inexperienced information seekers than finding the same information on the Internet using a "simple" search engine. On the other hand, computers and the Internet make information seeking and literacy improvement more difficult because they assume a number of new operational and formal skills. This adds an extra barrier to the skills of reading and writing.

Additionally, digital media require particular information, communication, content creation, and strategic skills that partially differ from those needed for the use of traditional media. Without such skills, one drowns in the vast ocean of information and other sources provided by the digital media. In our view, all of these skills taken together likely increase the gap between people with different educational, occupational, and age backgrounds in the new media compared to the traditional media.

We will show that operational and formal skills can "easily" be learned in language and computer classes, on-the-job training, or even personal practice. However, information, communication, content creation, and strategic skills are not learned "automatically" or simply by practice. The information skills that are necessary for the extremely vast and complex environment of the Internet and the communication skills needed for online social media are barely addressed at schools. Strategic skills, defined as being able to use media as the means for specific goals and for the general goals of improving one's position in society, are only trained in a particular job and school environments where computers and the Internet are used to attain particular neatly circumscribed goals. Where else should one learn systematic information retrieval on the Internet for one's particular personal or professional purposes? Where should one become familiar with the use of an online voting guide? Where can one be taught to search for friends on a social networking site? Where should one learn the strategies of online dating?

The creation of personal profiles, Tweets, and various wikis is partly preprogrammed and seems to be quite simple. The same is true for uploading user-generated content to various public websites and knowledge exchange networks. However, a critical observation of the results of these contributions to the web raises doubts as to their quality and effectiveness, at least from the view of a professional.

The Importance of Digital Skills

In this book, we will argue that the level of digital skills is one of the main factors in the explanation of digital media use (the other main factor is motivation.) People with adequate skills use computers and the Internet more frequently and for longer periods of time and use a variety of applications.

The extension of digital media use enables more and better participation in contemporary society in several fields. In the 2005 book *The Deepening Divide*, one of the authors of this book argued that the main advantages of having access to and skills for digital media were economic, social, political, cultural, educational and institutional, or citizen participation in society. Now, seven years later, this argument has become even more evident. Digital media have become a part of daily life. Computer use is less of a lifestyle option; it has increasingly become an everyday necessity. Living without such media is becoming increasingly difficult, as one would miss a growing number of opportunities. On several occasions, one would even be excluded from vital resources.

In chapter 3, we will discuss the impact of digital skills on various types of participation in society. We will also show that the disadvantages of not having access to the digital media and the inability to work with them are high. These stakes simply mean participation or exclusion from future society.

Conclusions

This chapter defines digital skills as a crucial phase in the appropriation of digital technology. People need sufficient motivation to acquire digital media and, subsequently, the motivation to learn the skills to use them. Only after performing these skills are they able to benefit from digital media use.

In this book, we prefer the concept of digital skills instead of, for example, digital literacy or information literacy. Literacy primarily refers to reading and writing, and information denotes knowledge. However, using digital media, such as the Internet, is more than the primarily mental operation of reading, writing, and gaining knowledge. It also involves (inter)active operations of working with hardware and software, communicating with people, and performing transactions of goods or services. Many more skills have to be performed than simply reading and writing.

In this chapter, a framework of six digital skills is introduced. The first are the medium-related skills, consisting of operational skills (technical competencies to command digital media) and formal skills (browsing and navigating, above all on the web). These skills are specific to each medium. The other four digital skills are content-related. They are similar to skills needed in most media, although they appear to have unique forms in digital media. Content-related digital skills are information skills (the ability to search, select, and evaluate information in digital media), communication skills (mostly on the Internet), content skills (user-generated content on the Internet), and strategic skills (using a digital medium as a means to achieving a particular personal or professional goal). The six medium- and content-related skills are presented here in a particular order because they have a conditional and sequential nature (content-related skills require medium-related skills, and the mastery of medium-related skills alone is not sufficient). To demonstrate that all six skills have similarities and differences when comparing traditional media, such as print and audiovisual media with digital media, we have compared them in boxes 1.1 and 1.2.

Contemporary, traditional, and digital skills are merely the latest media skills people have developed. A snapshot of history shows that an expanding and cumulative number of skills have appeared and that an ever-larger section of the population requires these skills. Today, the Internet requires more skills than traditional media and more than computer skills alone. For example, skills are needed when people search for information on the web, when they have to practice online communication, and when they create online content. On the one hand, computers and the Internet and their clever interfaces make such uses easier than traditional media. On the other hand, they make such uses more difficult because they involve learning additional skills. Those able to learn these skills will have the best opportunities to participate in present and future society.

Further Reading

- Van Dijk, J. A. G. M. (2005). The deepening divide: Inequality in the information society. Thousand Oaks, CA: Sage.
  Conceptual background of digital skills and explores how these skills are related to new media use and society.
- Potter, W. J. (2012). *Media Literacy (Sixth Edition)*. Thousand Oaks, CA: Sage.
  A broader concept of literacy by focusing on traditional media and normative accounts (critical insights of media contents and societal practices).
- Potter, W. J. (2004). *Theory of Media Literacy: A Cognitive Approach.* Thousand Oaks, CA: Sage.
  A more narrow approach by focusing on media knowledge instead of media practice or use.
- Livingstone, S., Van Couvering, E., & Thumim, N. (2008). Converging traditions of research on media and information literacies: Disciplinary, critical and methodological issues. In D. J. Leu, J. Coiro, M. Knobel, & C. Lankshear (Eds.), *Handbook of research on new literacies* (pp. 103–132). Mahwah, NJ: Lawrence Erlbaum Associates.
  Conceptual and research issues of the differences and similarities of media literacies and information or digital literacies.
- Lankshear, C., & Knobel, M. (2008). *Digital Literacies: Concepts, Policies and Practices.* New York; Washington, DC: Peter Lang.
  Collection of several diverging essays about issues related to digital literacies.
- Mizrach, S. (1998). From orality to teleliteracy. Available at: http:www.fiu.edu/~mizrachs/orality.htm.
  An overview of media skills in history.

CHAPTER 2

Defining Internet Skills

Introduction

In the first chapter, we introduced a list of the following digital skills: operational, formal, information, communication, content creation, and strategic skills. These skills were applied to several media. In this chapter, this range of skills is further elaborated in the context of the Internet, including World Wide Web services like email, social networking, and online telephony. To investigate the list of skills applied to the Internet, we develop a number of specific skill indices for all six skills. These indices are extracted from concepts related to Internet skills that are proposed in the last decades. The diversity of these concepts originates from a wide research scope, covering studies of media and communication, technology and computing, literacy, education, and information science.

Several synonymously and interchangeably used concepts, such as digital literacy, computer literacy (synonyms: information technology and electronic literacy), information literacy, network literacy (synonyms: Internet and hypermedia literacy), digital literacy (synonym: digital information literacy), and media literacy can be identified (Bawden, 2001, 2008). Some of these definitions prove more useful than others; they range from abilities to use the Internet to cultural ideals such as economic development or personal fulfillment (Tyner, 1998). Furthermore, often the exact nature of the concepts remains inadequately defined and no theoretical justification is provided. Many of the earlier concepts that focus specifically on the Internet considered primarily basic skills such as navigating, searching for information, or downloading files (e.g., Bunz, 2004, 2009; Hargittai, 2002; Potosky, 2007). Other scholars avoided narrow definitions and combined concepts to explain what is needed to use the Internet. Warschauer (2003), for example, considered computer literacy (defined in terms of the basic forms of computer and network operation), information literacy (the ability to manage vast amounts of information), multimedia literacy (the ability to understand and produce multimedia content), and computer-mediated communication literacy (the skill of effectively managing online communications such as email, chatting, videoconferencing, and the ability to adhere to the rules of "netiquette"). Eshet-Alkalai (2004) considered digital literacy to involve more than the mere ability to use software or operate a digital device. Her concept includes photo visual literacy ("reading" instructions from graphical displays), reproduction literacy (utilizing digital reproduction to create new, meaningful materials from preexisting materials), information literacy (evaluating the quality and validity of information), branching literacy (constructing knowledge from nonlinear, hypertextual navigation), and socioemotional literacy (understanding the "rules" that prevail in cyberspace and applying this understanding in online cyberspace communication). Such combinations and integrations of literacy concepts correspond with the migration of social interactions toward the Internet. A related skill added more recently is the ability to communicate with others on social networking sites (e.g., Lankshear & Knobel, 2011).

In this book and particularly in this chapter, we propose a definition for Internet skills that accounts for the latest affordances such as social networking. The proposed definition focuses on how the general Internet user can receive most of the benefits from the Internet environment, whether they are online on smartphone, tablet, or laptop. To apply and elaborate on the framework proposed in chapter 1, we investigate a variety of related concepts that exist. The variety of concepts suggests that several approaches for adding skills indices to the proposed framework are possible, all with their own strengths and weaknesses. By using the framework proposed in chapter 1 as a point of departure, a one-sided technological viewpoint is avoided. Both technical aspects that are linked to the use of the Internet (apparent in the operational and formal skills) and substantive aspects that are related to the content provided by the Internet (included in the information, communication, content creation, and strategic skills) are included. Each of the six Internet skills will now be discussed in greater detail.

Operational Skills

In 1981, soon after the popularization of the personal computer, a concept that elaborated the special skills required for the use of computers was invented and published in the Washington Post (Warschauer, 2003). The term was computer literacy, a narrow concept that indicated basic forms of computer operation such as turning on a computer, opening a folder, and saving a file. Unfortunately, such narrow definitions of skills required for computer use remained customary for a long time. In educational contexts, computer literacy often resulted in tool-oriented approaches, which limited teaching to relatively trivial software instruction (Hoem & Schwebs, 2004). Other terms used to indicate a set of basic skills in utilizing computer or Internet technology are technical competence (Mossberger, Tolbert, & Stansbury, 2003), technological literacy (Carvin, 2000), and technical proficiency (Søby, 2003). According to Carvin, technological literacy is the ability to utilize common information technology (IT) tools, including hardware, software, and Internet tools such as search engines and email. Søby describes technical proficiency as the basic component of digital literacy, including a foundational knowledge of hardware, software, applications, networks, and elements of digital technology. Similarly, IT and ICT literacy, in most cases, cover the basic skills to use computers and networks. In chapter 1, we followed these descriptions by defining operational skills as the technical competencies required to command media. In popular language, they are called "button knowledge." We consider operational skills as the most basic skills that one should possess before one is able to demonstrate other skills.

In this section, we will elaborate the operational skills that are required to use Internet services. We define operational skills that are required to use Internet services regardless of the device on which they are accessed (e.g., desktop computers, laptops, smartphones, handheld PDAs, or tablet PCs). The skills necessary to operate Internet services are addressed in several measurements (e.g., Bunz, 2004, 2009; Larsson, 2002; Potosky, 2007). Bunz (2004, 2009) investigated so-called web fluency by using a survey instrument that considered opening Web addresses, identifying host servers from Web addresses, using "back" and "forward" buttons to move between webpages and using search engines. Larsson (2002) created a Digital Literacy Checklist. Examples of the operational skill-related items include knowing how to use a web browser and use it to move between websites or pages, using the browser's bookmark file to organize websites, changing the browser's preferences, emptying disk and memory cache on the browser to free up space, reading various file formats on the web, downloading (and/or listening to) audio files, identifying online file formats and knowing how to move files to the desktop for further analysis, and downloading files using a web browser.

To define operational skills for the Internet, we not only focus on using websites but also on online services and applications (apps) that are used by the large majority (e.g., email, social networking sites, and online telephony). We neglect operations that are not a direct requisite to use the Internet. The operational Internet skills are defined in a rather broad manner to comprise popular information and communication Internet services.

First, we consider the basic use of Internet services, which requires *recognizing and operating toolbars, buttons, and menus*. Without the skills to use these operators, one cannot open a website in an Internet browser, open a received email message, or open an application. Furthermore, when using online telephony, one must know how to respond to and place a call. Toolbars, buttons, and menus come in many forms and, unfortunately, often do not follow standardized design guidelines. Even when they serve the same purpose, buttons might look different between one Internet browser and another or between different mobile online services and applications. Buttons' users should certainly be familiar with those available in Internet browsers, such as the toolbar buttons of Back and Forward and the Home button. Other helpful buttons include refreshing webpages or bookmarking websites. For operating email, knowledge of other specific buttons is required, such as Send, Receive, Reply, and Forward.

The second group of operational skills includes *using different types of user input options* found in various Internet services. Online forms offer various types of input fields (e.g., text boxes, pull-down menus, list boxes) that people must be familiar with to fill them. These input fields can be found in many services, with the most prominent being the search engine. A user should not only recognize the search engine on a website but also know to click in the search box to indicate the wish to enter a search query and then

Box 2.1   Operational Internet Skills

We consider operational Internet skills as the ability to

- Recognize and operate the Internet service's toolbars, buttons, and menus (e.g., opening a Website, navigating forward and backward by using browser buttons; opening, sending or receiving email; starting or accepting a call in online telephony, opening an application);
- Use different types of user input fields found in Internet services (e.g., input field in a search engine or other form, pull-down menus, or radio buttons);
- Manage different file formats opened or saved from Internet services (e.g., opening or saving a PDF file, sending a mail attachment, downloading photos or videos, or bookmarking websites).

hit the search button to begin the search process. He or she should also understand where to add an email address or type an email message.

Finally, we consider file management or the *opening and saving of various file formats* that can be found online. Websites or webpages can be managed in bookmarks, music and videos can be downloaded, and files can be received as attachments (e.g., in email, chat, or social networking) and subsequently opened or saved.

Box 2.1 provides an overview of the operational skills required for using the Internet. The use of the basic operations mentioned might sound quite straightforward; however, as we will show in the chapter 4, this is not the case for everyone.

Formal Skills

Gilster (1997) presented the idea that new media require new skills for both navigating networked technologies and interpreting the meaning of digital messages. The ability to navigate networked technologies is part of what we have termed formal skills. Every medium has particular formal characteristics that must be understood and requires techniques that must be mastered. Formal skills relate to the structures on which a medium is built. The Internet, and especially the web, is the most obvious example of hypermedia, requiring the skills of both browsing and navigating. Users must have these skills to use the vast and diverse number of online websites, platforms, and menu layouts offered. These layouts differ in (the placement of) text, content, backgrounds, photos, frames, links, buttons, and pop-ups. Furthermore, they differ in (traditional and more recent) features designed to help the user navigate: elements such as color of text and links; multimedia elements such as sound, animation, or video; and interactive features such as chats, forms, or message boards. Similar features account for the design of menus (e.g., static or rollover).

All of these distinct characteristics demand user navigational skills. Many online platforms or websites use features without sufficient attention to human factors, rendering these sites inaccessible to all but users with sophisticated know-how about Web navigation (Dimaggio & Hargittai, 2001). Often, websites seem to be usable from the perspective of the developers but perform rather poorly in usability tests. In this regard, studies typically assume a functional perspective in which the design of the website is tested. This helps to improve website functionality, but it neglects users' skills deficiencies.

Disorientation is a frequently cited problem in hypermedia use (Lee, 2005). Most traditional media are linear, giving the user little control over the flow of information. Hypermedia provide a formal structure that enables users to choose nonlinear paths rather than the fixed formal structures of print media, for example, chapters, paragraphs, and references (Kwan, 2001; Coiro & Dobler, 2007). Now, users can move forward, backward, to known and unknown locations and to other services (e.g., when clicking a link to a webpage in an email or chat service). The Internet offers a large and complex landscape and its hypermedia structure does not provide many spatial and navigational clues. Without a sense of location, distance and necessary direction, it is not surprising that users often experience a strong sense of disorientation (Kwan, 2001), which in turn might result in a loss of interest, frustration, and a decline in user efficiency (McDonald & Stevenson, 1998). It is important to note that getting lost on the Internet also occurs when users have sufficient domain expertise. Thus, disorientation should be framed in terms of structure, links, and design, independent of the information topics being navigated (Danielson, 2003; Webster & Ahuja, 2006). For this reason, we consider medium-related skills to include formal skills. An important set of skills, given that the structure of the Internet changes continually; pages appear, reappear, or disappear. As the Internet continues to grow, the complexity of this medium continues to increase.

Formal skills for the Internet are the skills needed to use different website layouts and maintain one's orientation when surfing on and between websites. They are also required when navigating through the various categories in web directories, search result lists, lists of friends on social networking

---

Box 2.2   Formal Internet Skills

We consider formal Internet skills as the ability to

- Navigate the Internet by
  - Using hyperlinks embedded in different formats such as texts, images, menus, emails, or applications.
- Maintain a sense of location while navigating, meaning
  - Not becoming disoriented when navigating within a website or online platform;
  - Not becoming disoriented when navigating between websites or online platforms;
  - Not becoming disoriented when opening and browsing through lists, such as search results, online discussions, personal profiles, emails, or contacts.

sites, posted messages in online discussion groups, or lists with email messages. The formal Internet skills are listed in box 2.2.

Information Skills

There is no doubt that the importance and the amount of information have spectacularly increased over the last few decades. Information (re)production has become the major form of earning a living for large segments of society. Thus, coping with the massive amounts of available information and the supporting technologies is important for all individuals. In chapter 1, we defined information skills as the ability to search information, select relevant information, process the information, and evaluate the information found. In digital media, we can observe information skills regarding computers, telephones, and other types of digital media that provide information. Most imperative, however, are the information skills concerning the Internet. After all, "the fundamental principle behind the Internet was that once someone somewhere made available a document, database, graphic, sound, video or screen at some stage in an interactive dialogue, it should be accessible by anyone, with any type of computer, in any country" (Berners-Lee & Fischetti, 2000, p. 37). The Internet has made it easier than ever for individuals and organizations to publish information to a potentially large audience.

Before the diffusion of the Internet in households, searches within electronic databases were typically facilitated by individuals who were skilled in the use of databases, such as librarians (Jenkins, Corritore, & Wiedenbeck, 2003). Because of the ubiquity of the Internet and search engines, most users have not received formal training in the use of search facilities (Thatcher, 2008). Searching skills are commonly subsumed under information literacy and digital literacy. Standards and statements regarding these terms are produced by several professional information associations. However, much confusion exists around these concepts and many other concepts have been suggested (e.g., infoliteracy, informacy, information empowerment, information competence, and information mediacy). The literature relevant to information Internet skills is spread across different areas. These areas tend to remain separate, causing a poor integration of information retrieval science (Jenkins et al., 2003). Overall, most of the literature seems to focus on the search for (online) information—an action by which users attempt to fulfill their information needs. It is generally agreed that this process of searching entails more than merely gathering information; it also encompasses posing or identifying a question or problem, exploring available information, refining the question, gathering and evaluating information, and synthesizing and using information (Wallace, Kupperman, Krajcik, & Soloway, 2000).

Because our goal is to provide a definition of information Internet skills, we follow this agreement and focus on studies that adopt a stage approach in explaining the search process. In this regard, Marchionini (1995) proposed a distinction that was originally developed in the context of traditional information retrieval. It is, however, still generally accepted and appropriate for digital environments such as the Internet. The distinction is recursive and not solely limited to the information-seeking process in search engines. Many scholars of online searching have adapted aspects of this framework. The process entails problem definition, choosing a source, defining search queries, selecting information, and evaluating information (see also box 2.3 at the end of this section). We will utilize this distinction as our point of departure for analyzing information skills.

Defining the Information Problem

The search process begins with a problem definition. The identification of an information need can be regarded as the determination or definition of a problem (Brand-Gruwel, Wopereis, & Vermetten, 2005). To create a comprehensive problem definition, a clear description and the type and amount of information required to solve the information problem are required.

Choosing a Website or a Search System to Seek Information

Once the information problem has been formulated, sources of information to use in solving the problem should be considered. For searching on the Internet, people have many options (e.g., specialized websites, search engines, meta-search tools, directories, or several specialized resources). The value of online sources of information is based on criteria such as reliability, validity, precision, completeness, accuracy, availability, novelty, and costs (Brand-Gruwel et al., 2005).

Defining Search Queries

The third step, formulating search queries, has gained considerable attention in academic research. The next chapter will describe several related problems that users experience in this step. These problems severely hinder the online search process because the following steps largely depend on the quality of the search queries defined.

Selecting Information

For the fourth step, selecting the most relevant information or search results, people must be able to separate relevant from irrelevant search results. When a search engine only returns a few results, they can all be inspected. However, when people use broad searching strategies in tandem with large-scale search engines, a vast number of unsuitable results will appear (Livingstone, Van Couvering, & Thumim, 2005). This problem might be reinforced when people who are searching for information only select the first few search results or do not venture past the first page of search results.

Evaluating Information

The final step is the ability to make informed judgments about what is found via an Internet connection, or what Gilster (1997) referred to as "the art of critical thinking." Information is not always of the same quality. The large diversity of quality of online information requires the skills of evaluation. Alexander and Tate (1999) identified the following five criteria in an analysis of print texts as applied to webpages: accuracy, authority, objectivity, currency, and coverage. It is necessary to examine these criteria to verify the reliability of the sources. This examination is key in evaluating most of the new media and creates a need for citizens to acquire new capabilities related to assessing the value, veracity, and reliability of information if they are to effectively participate in a global society (Mansell, 2002). Related to this step in the search process is the concept of media literacy, which was developed from the critical evaluation of mass media. Originally, media literacy was meant to be a protection from what many people perceived as the treacherous effects of mass media (Martin, 2006).

Box 2.3 Information Internet Skills

We consider information Internet skills as the ability to

- Locate required information by
  - Defining the information problem;
  - Choosing a Website or a search system to seek information;
  - Defining search options or queries;
  - Selecting information (on websites or in search results);
  - Evaluating information sources.

Communication Skills

In chapter 1, we defined communication skills as the ability to encode and decode messages to construct, understand, and exchange meaning. In digital media, we can observe communication skills in the use of computers, telephones, the Internet, and other instances of digital media. In computers, communication occurs between humans and technical artifacts, hardware, and software. Therefore, we defined computer communication skills as the exchange of meaning through interaction with computer interfaces and software. In telephones, communication occurs between humans via a technical central exchange system. On the Internet, communication is realized by humans with artifacts, such as the information repositories of websites, and with other humans in the growing number of types of message exchange in this medium. Therefore, we defined communication Internet skills as the ability to encode and decode messages to construct, understand, and exchange meaning in all interactive applications of the Internet. These interactions can be both with artifacts such as websites, search engines and other Internet software, and with other humans using message systems such as email, chatboxes, and instant messaging. Interaction with Internet artifacts was discussed in the former information skills section. In this section, we will focus on communication in the narrower sense of interaction with other people via the Internet.

In the first two decades of its history, the Internet was predominantly a medium for information retrieval. Although email was one of the main applications from the start, the focus was on consulting websites. After the turn of the century, the Internet began evolving into a principal communication medium, among others, by the rise of the so-called social media. The majority of Internet use is now dedicated to communication. The number of Internet communication services grows each year. The following services, and the skills required to effectively use them, will be discussed in this section:

- World Wide Web
- Email
- Chatboxes and instant messaging
- Internet telephony (such as Skype)
- Weblogs
- Twitter ("micro-blogging")
- Social networking sites

- Online dating
- Peer-to-peer networking (knowledge exchange)
- Virtual social worlds (such as Second Life)
- Virtual communities
- Collective online games

To call such services a communication service indicates that an exchange of messages with meaning encoded by a sender and decoded by receivers is a regular part of the service. Preprogrammed music-, photo-, and video-exchange sites and collective online games without additional messages in the form of comments, tags, or captions will be excluded here.

We consider the communication Internet skills as listed in box 2.4. The ten communication skills are ordered from basic to more advanced skills. More advanced skills reveal more strategic aspects. This is evident in attracting attention online and constructing profiles, which require both communication skills and strategic skills: What is the Internet user attempting to achieve?

Box 2.4   Communication Internet Skills

We consider communication Internet skills as the ability to

- Search, select, evaluate, and act upon contacts online (networking).
- Encode messages online: Construct meaning.
- Decode messages online: Understand meaning.
- Exchange messages online: Exchange meaning.
- Attract attention online.
- Profile online identities.
- Performance: The ability to adopt alternative online identities for discovery or improvisation.
- Play and simulation: The capacity of online experimentation for better decision-making.
- Collective intelligence: The social ability to pool knowledge and exchange meaning with others in peer-to-peer networking.
- Negotiation: The ability to exchange meaning to reach decisions and realize transactions while understanding the meanings of others/ partners.

Search, Select, Evaluate and Act upon
Contacts Online (Networking)

Communication skills begin with making and maintaining contacts. In a large number of applications, the Internet multiplies the number of contacts people have. Many people experience problems managing this multitude. Internet services offer many opportunities for networking that were previously unavailable. To benefit from these opportunities, one must have online networking skills. These skills require a more explicit number of subsequent steps than do the skills of face-to-face networking. They comprise a number of operational and formal skills to search, select, and react to contacts in a particular service, such as email, chatboxes, and social networking sites. Without these skills, one will be flooded by the large number of potential contacts. Further, these skills consist of a number of information, communication, and strategic skills that help to continually evaluate these contacts and treat them in a goal-oriented manner. However, explicit these skills may be, they are rarely taught. This is evident in email skills. Many people, both workers and consumers, are quite inefficient in using email, making it an important source of loss of productivity in organizations.

A second Internet service that strongly requires the command of contact management is social networking sites. The creation, expansion, maintenance, and reduction of so-called friends in these sites are a necessary communication skill in using these sites.

A third example of a service that requires skills of contact management is online dating. In this case, contact management is the prime activity, that is, the ability to acquire, organize, and complete dates for potential partnership. Many online daters are very selective in making contacts. When they have found a suitable candidate, they need the communication skills to address this person in a convincing way ("online flirting"). When the dating process fails, they need the communication skills to end it appropriately. Although a large part of this process is preprogrammed and many contact aids are offered, a successful dating process requires a large number of individual skills. In fact, this is a general characteristic of all Internet services discussed in this section. Despite preprogramming, these services require user skills. Therefore, preprogramming is often misleading, as developers and users of these services believe that all individuals are able to use them. This again explains why so few guides and courses for this type of communication skills are offered.

Encode Messages Online: Construct Meaning

Communication on the Internet requires the ability to speak and write. Applications with touchscreens, pictures, and sounds that can be used by illiterates are not particularly numerous (see chapter 6 for the special problems of illiterates regarding digital skills). In speaking and writing, one is able to benefit from the abilities developed in traditional media. However, more is needed in several of these applications. First, one must take into account the nature of the new medium. The structure and style of an email typically differs from those of a traditional letter. Short Message Service (SMS) and chat have developed a special type of language that is full of abbreviations and surrogate words that are only known to the (mainly young) users who have created them. Twitter only allows expressions of 140 characters and caters to people who excel in one-liners.

A second major new skill needed to encode messages in an increasing number of Internet services is the skill to use multimedia. Users not only need to write texts but must also process pictures, graphics, videos, and audio-messages. Appropriate combinations of these symbol systems in multimedia messages and collages are a required skill in the multimedia world. However, learning to use multimedia is rarely taught in regular education.

Decode Messages Online: Understand Meaning

For reading and understanding messages, the same conclusions regarding writing and encoding can be drawn. The ability of good reading developed for texts is a prime requirement for good communication Internet skills. However, more is needed to understand the meaning of new media messages. Email messages are often taken literally and rationally, although they have been written in a rush and driven by emotions. For new SMS and chatbox users, parts of the writing encountered are a type of secret writing. Understanding multimedia messages might be quite difficult for seniors who did not grow up using them. Often, they consider the over-crowded and steeply changing multimedia screens as overly difficult to process.

Exchange Messages Online: Exchange Meaning

In asynchronous Internet applications such as email, Twitter, social networking sites, and online dating, many users do not know how and how quickly they should react to a previous message. Parallel nonverbal signs showing the importance and urgency of a message are missing. Habits of online response time are only beginning to be established. In peer-to-peer networking and online forums, many people do not know when and how to post a particular contribution, as expectations are typically far from clear.

This is one of the reasons why many individuals do not actively participate in these online groups and instead only consume their contents. In online dating, the exchange of meaning is vital. It causes the dating process to succeed or fail. When online daters lack the skills of "online flirting" or getting to know each other over the Internet, eventual physical meetings might turn into a disappointment.

In synchronous Internet applications such as chatboxes, instant messaging, direct peer-to-peer networking, and virtual social worlds, participants must know how to behave as communicators. Internet conversation often lacks politeness; it is short, direct, and abrupt. It might even turn into rude, insulting, aggressive, and inflammatory language known as flaming. So-called netiquette is a mode of online behavior that must be learned in practice, as virtually no guidance in courses or regular education is available.

Attract Attention Online

One of the most important communication skills people need on the Internet is to attract attention with their messages, profiles, and identities. It is easy to speak on the Internet, but it is difficult to be heard (Hindman, 2009). The vast majority of expressions on the web simply have no or very few receivers. A large portion of personal websites has no visitors. A great portion of postings to online forums has no readership. The bulk of Twitter messages simply disappear into thin air. The authors cannot control the lack of receivers. It is a structural limitation of the Internet that expressions are so easily made on this medium and average reception is limited by default. To stand out, Internet authors require the skills of a journalist or a politician, excelling in one-liners. Few common users have these skills. They are not taught and can only be developed through personal talent.

Construct Online Profiles and Identities

The importance of online profiles and identities is steadily growing in our individualized network society (Van Dijk, 2006). Social networking sites, online dating, and virtual worlds have become much more important. These services require some form of impression management. Users must create personal profiles and representatives such as avatars. Social networking sites, online dating sites, and virtual worlds offer their users many aids in creating a profile or an avatar. Facebook and online dating sites suggest preprogrammed personal profiles. The result is a gray average of profiles and few conspicuous profiles that attract attention.

Performance: The Ability to Adopt Alternative Online Identities for Discovery or Improvisation

The previously mentioned six communication skills are skills that every Internet user should possess to effectively use Internet services. The same is true for attracting attention and building personal profiles. The following four communication Internet skills cannot be expected to be commanded by average users. They are advanced skills that people need for a higher level of participation in the online world. They are inspired by the list of new skills of participatory online culture proposed by Jenkins, Purushotma, Weigel, Clinton, and Robinson (2009).

Online profiles and identities are not created in a single act; they are built while interacting with others who provide feedback. The capacity to adequately respond to feedback and to be inspired by the profiles and identities of others is an important communication skill on the Internet. Especially children, teens, and adolescents enjoy experimenting with virtual identities to create and learn to understand their original physical and mental identities. Various types of play with online identities are used to test and discover their own evolving identities, experiment with possible selves, and explore the unknown social spaces of other young people and adults (Jenkins et al., 2009). Compared to seniors, young people are typically advanced in these skills, as they are part of their personal growth path. However, even young people must learn these skills and correct many pitfalls in the making of their online identity, especially when they are confronted by people with harmful intentions.

Play and Simulation: The Capacity of Online Experimentation for Better Decision-Making

The Internet offers a growing number of game- or simulation-like applications that can be used for learning and preparations of decision-making offline. Games are an important tool, especially for young people to learn, explore, and process knowledge and make decisions (Jenkins et al., 2009). Particularly, serious collective online games, which require certain social skills, can be valuable learning tools. The skills needed to use serious games and simulations can be learned in practice or by trial and error, with the exception of the most difficult applications. Individuals who do not enjoy playing or who have not developed the skills of communication or interaction in playing with others may experience problems.

Collective Intelligence: The Social Ability to Pool Knowledge and Exchange Meaning with Others in Peer-to-Peer Networking

In the peer-to-peer networking of online knowledge communities and other cooperative networks, information and experience are exchanged. This exchange requires the skills of online cooperation, which primarily rest on communication. The exchange requires "the ability to identify specific functions for each member based on his or her expertise and to interact with the team members in an appropriate fashion" (Jenkins et al., 2009, p. 76). These competencies are becoming increasingly important in contemporary workplaces. However, they are scarcely learned in current formal education. Currently, formal education focuses on individual skills and autonomous personal, rather than collective, problem solving. Thus, these online cooperation skills must be learned in practice, leading to inequalities in the development of these skills. Strikingly, present-day children, teens, and adolescents learn the skills on their own initiative in their online culture of massive exchange of nearly everything. The discrepancy between this autonomous learning of young people and their education in schools grows daily (Buckingham, 2012).

Negotiation: The Ability to Exchange Meaning to Reach Decisions and Realize Transactions while Understanding the Meanings of Others/Partners

The last communication skill to be discussed is the art of online negotiation. It is practiced in various virtual communities, peer-to-peer networking, email exchanges, ecommerce transactions and, of course, online dating. Negotiation requires high level of communication skills. The demands of negotiation skills in the online world increase as social and cultural differences increase.

Many observers believe that only similar people interact in homogeneous communities of interest on the Internet. However, there is an increasing degree of heterogeneity in online communication because the Internet reinforces long-distance and international communication and joins groups that would have no direct contact in the physical world. "In such a world, it becomes increasingly critical to help students acquire skills in understanding multiple perspectives, respecting and even embracing diversity of views, understanding a variety of social norms and negotiating between conflicting opinions" (Jenkins et al., 2009, p. 99). This environment requires social and communication skills that help in listening to and responding to a range of different perspectives. These types of skills are only informally learned in schools, workplaces, and communities that are socially and culturally heterogeneous.

Content Creation Skills

Information Internet skills are required to locate information produced and uploaded by others. Communication Internet skills are required to utilize Internet content to construct, understand, and exchange meaning. Content creation skills are required to create content of acceptable quality to be published on the Internet. The Internet requires user-generated content such as websites, weblogs, bulletin boards, news groups, chat forums, videos, and music. The essential notions of literacy ranges from critically consuming content to using tools of content creation.

There are many aids available that help people create and publish content online. Various tools facilitate the posting of content, even by users who lack technical skills. These tools are becoming increasingly accessible to the general Internet user. Today, videos shot on photo cameras or mobile phones can be uploaded and posted on YouTube without considering compression details or pixel qualities. Furthermore, it is not necessary to understand programming languages to post on a personal blog or website. Any restrictions imposed on users in terms of hardware and software seem to be decreasing continuously. Thus, the creation of online content is far less complex and time-consuming than it was in the past. However, this advance also makes information and communication Internet skills all the more vital in the online environment. The increasing amounts of online content not only place extra stress on the information Internet skill of evaluation, but they also make it much more difficult to be heard or to stand out with the aid of communication skills.

The availability of various types of content creation tools has resulted in a large variety of quality of the online content produced. The skills to create online content might be relatively well developed for traditional written resources, but the use of tools to create "eloquent" digital content leaves much room for improvement.

The online variety in the quality of written texts, photos, and videos is large. Unfortunately, low-quality creations might hinder or corrupt the intention or purpose of the created content. Only especially funny or newsworthy online videos and other postings permit the lack of quality.

Although many tools seem quite simple to use, creating attractive and proper content of high quality remains unachievable for many users. The ability to create high-quality videos or photos is more important to some users than others. However, in general, the quality of the created content should be sufficient to achieve the intended goal of the creation. Content creation suggests a high level of Internet communication skills because the purpose of created content in most cases is sharing. This section focuses on the creation of online content of acceptable quality. The actual creator's message is part of communication and strategic skills.

In chapter 1, we defined content creation skills as the ability to create contributions to the Internet of a specific type that requires a particular plan or design, for example, a personal website or video. In addition, we consider the skills to remix content, which is defined as combining existing pieces of content to create a new piece of content, as an addition to creating original content (Lenhart, Purcell, Smith, & Zickuhr, 2010). Basically, remixing refers to merging material found online (such as text, images, music, and videos) into a new creation.

User-generated content covers a broad range of technologies such as blogging, video, and photo postings from mobile devices, podcasting, or contributing to wikis. Likewise, it covers a series of different services. For example, there are many possible ways of compressing or storing videos and images for the web. Overall, the process of content creation entails the steps of creating content in the form of text, video, photo, music, or multimedia. The created content may arise in many different forms. It can be published on a personal website, video sites such as YouTube, social networking sites, online gaming sites, or on other sites. See box 2.5 for the definition of content creation Internet Skills.

Content creation skills may be learned on an amateur or professional level. The vast majority of contributions on the web demonstrate an amateur level. This is acceptable if the result is effective or attractive to receivers. However, many amateur contributions lack quality and are not effective in terms of the goal of senders and receivers. A minimum level of quality indicates that texts do not contain substantial mistakes such that they cannot be read by receivers or can only be read with the greatest difficulty. Videos lack quality when they are sweeping, marked by fits and starts, twists or turns, and tilts. Photos are unlikely to be appreciated when they are blurry, out of focus, or have framing issues. Effective and attractive content suggests that the created content has the intended or perhaps unsolicited effect of senders on receivers and is attractive to these receivers regardless of quality level. In discussing the goals of senders and users in information retrieval, communication, and content creation, we transition to strategic skills.

Box 2.5 Content creation Internet Skills

We consider content creation Internet skills as the skills required to

- Create proper (minimum quality level) and effective or attractive
  - Textual content;
  - Music and video content;
  - Photo or image content;
  - Multimedia content;
  - Remixed content.

Strategic Skills

Van Dijk (2005) defines strategic skills as the capacity to use computer and network sources as the means of reaching particular goals and for the general goal of improving one's position in society. Strategic skills are considered to be the most advanced Internet skills. To receive the greatest benefit of the Internet, users require a high degree of information, communication, and content creation skills. Then, they are able to perform strategic skills, which include decision-making. What is the individual going to do with the information gathered? What was the purpose of the online conversation or collaboration? What does one hope to accomplish with a personal creation such as a blog or video? To acquire strategic skills and employ them on the Internet, users must be critical and analytical.

Few skill-related studies explicitly address strategic Internet skills. In this chapter, a process that consists of four analytically distinct steps in making effective use of the Internet is proposed. The process of decision-making employed to introduce a definition of strategic skills has its origin in the classical approach to decision-making, which emphasizes the procedures through which decision-makers can reach an optimal solution as efficiently as possible (Miller, 2006). Box 2.6 at the end of this section lists the strategic skills indices.

Developing an Orientation toward a Particular Goal

The first step in the decision-making process is goal orientation. In this context, goal orientation refers to awareness of the opportunities offered by the Internet and subsequently determining the goal of the Internet session. Focusing on this goal and working toward it is difficult, especially in a digital media landscape that offers a large number of distracting stimuli (e.g., the many advertisements and banners on the Internet, the continuous offer of hyperlinks to click on, and the many places to communicate, create profiles, or post a personal creation). Users must be aware of the goal of the Internet session.

Taking the Correct Action to Reach This Goal

The second step in the decision-making process is taking the correct actions on the Internet. In correspondence with the decision-making process, this step refers to gathering and combining various online information sources to achieve the best means of reaching the desired goal (Miller, 2006). The actions also include the choice of an online channel to optimize the chance of reaching the set goals. For example, in locating the hospital with the shortest waiting list for a specific medical treatment, one should not blindly follow a recommendation gathered from an online forum or solely take into account the information provided on the website of one specific hospital. This step entails many choices to be made on the Internet such as choosing the best place to publish created content.

Making the Right Decision to Reach This Goal

After the correct actions are taken, decisions must be made regarding how to reach the original goal by using the (often-excessive amount of) retrieved information and communication outcomes selectively; this is the third step. In the decision-making process, this step refers to developing a set of decision options and evaluating them according to carefully developed criteria (Miller, 2006). The decision-making process ends when an optimal decision is identified and decision implementation can begin (Miller, 2006).

Box 2.6   Strategic Creation Internet Skills

We reflect on the following indicators of strategic Internet skills:

- Developing an orientation toward a particular goal;
- Taking the correct actions to reach this goal;
- Making the right decisions to reach this goal; and eventually
- Gaining the benefits that result from the goal.

Gaining the Benefits that Result from the Goal

The final step is that of obtaining the benefits from making the optimal decision. These benefits can be of an economic, political, social, health, or cultural nature. As described in the first chapter, in all of these domains, Internet use can have beneficial outcomes.

Conclusions

In this chapter, the six digital skills proposed in chapter 1 are further elaborated in terms of the Internet. The proposed definition of Internet skills is based on individual abilities. These skills are a requirement of socially accepted and effective Internet use. They are relevant for the general population to function well in an increasingly digital environment. The six skills categories are divided into both medium- (operational and formal) and content-related (information, communication, content creation, and strategic) skills. By accounting for both technical aspects related to the use of the Internet and substantive aspects related to the content provided on the Internet, a technologically deterministic interpretation of Internet skills is avoided. The presented concept of Internet skills is of a sequential and conditional nature in the way that content-related skills depend on medium-related skills. This lead to the framework presented in figure 2.1 for measuring Internet skills.

Further Reading

- Bawden, ·D. (2008). Origins and concepts of digital literacy. In C. Lankshear & M. Knobel (Eds.), *Digital literacies: Concepts, policies & practices* (pp. 17–32). New York: Peter Lang.
  How the idea of digital literacy emerged and developed and how it relates to various other literacies.
- Jenkins, H., Purushotma, R., Weigel, M., Clinton, K., & Robinson, A. J. (2009). *Confronting the challenges of participatory culture. Media education for the 21st century.* Cambridge, MA: The MIT Press.
  Describes a new culture emerging from the use of participatory media, which requires new skills.
- Buckingham, D. (2012). *Beyond technology: Children's learning in the age of digital culture.* Cambridge: Polity.
  An analysis of learning, young people, and digital media.

Operational Internet skills
- Recognize and operate the Internet service's toolbars, buttons, and menus;
- Use different types of user input fields found in Internet services;
- Manage different file formats opened or saved from Internet services.

Formal Internet Skills
- Navigate on the Internet by
  - Using hyperlinks embedded in different formats such as texts, images, or menus.
- Maintain a sense of location while navigating on the Internet, meaning
  - Not becoming disoriented when navigating within a website;
  - Not becoming disoriented when navigating between websites;
  - Not becoming disoriented when opening and browsing through search results.

Information Internet Skills
- Locate required information by
  - Defining the information problem;
  - Choosing a Website or a search system to seek information;
  - Defining search options or queries;
  - Selecting information (on websites or in search results);
  - Evaluating information sources.

Communication Internet Skills
- Communicate on the Internet by
  - Searching, selecting, evaluating, and acting upon contacts online (networking);
  - Encoding messages online: Construct meaning;
  - Decoding messages online: Understand meaning;
  - Exchanging messages online: Exchange meaning;
  - Attracting attention online;
  - Constructing online profiles and identities;
  - Adopting alternative online identities for discovery or improvisation;
  - Online experimentation for better decision-making;
  - Pooling knowledge and exchange meaning with others in peer-to-peer networking;
  - Negotiating: The ability to exchange meaning to reach decisions and realize transactions while understanding the meanings of others/partners.

Content creation Internet skills
- Create proper and effective or attractive
  - Textual content;
  - Music and video content;
  - Photo or image content;
  - Multimedia content;
  - Remixed content.

Strategic Internet skills
- Take advantage of the Internet by
  - Developing an orientation toward a particular goal;
  - Taking the correct action to reach this goal;
  - Making the right decision to reach this goal;
  - Gaining from the benefits that result from the goal.

Medium-related Internet skills

Content-related Internet skills

Figure 2.1 Framework of Six Types of Internet Skills.

CHAPTER 3

Impact: Why Digital Skills Are the Key to the Information Society

Introduction: The Social Context of Skills

In this book, we attempt to draw a broad social picture of the backgrounds and consequences of the digital skills as defined in the previous chapter while we have mainly focused on Internet skills. Although skills are often linked to training or education, we take a more social-scientific or sociological approach. We will show that solutions beyond those of an educational nature should be sought in addressing the problem of a lack of digital skills.

In education, people mainly focus on particular types of training, courses, programs, competencies, and curriculum development or they think about target groups and didactic approaches for the special type of education required here. We prefer to consider the causes of digital skill inequalities first and the consequences next. In the next chapter, we will address the social demographics of digital skill inequalities. This is a rather descriptive approach. Here, we take a further step by shortly introducing a theory that enables us to explain differential access to digital technologies and the skills of using these technologies, as will be observed in the performance tests discussed in chapter 4. This theory might also predict the consequences of unequal access and skills, which are the central topic of this chapter.

We have labeled our theory, Resources and Appropriation Theory (Van Dijk, 2005, 2012). This theory considers digital skills as a crucial part of the appropriation of information and communication technology. Appropriation involves a process with four phases, which were introduced in chapter 1: motivation, physical and material access, digital skills, and usage. Effective and satisfactory use of digital media cannot occur without sufficient motivation, access, and skills. The total process of appropriation is influenced by the social and technological context of digital media use. The social context consists of personal and positional social inequalities among users. In the following chapters, we will observe that skill differences relate to personal characteristics such as age, gender, and education and to social characteristics such as having a job, enrollment in school, and living in a social environment that stimulates the use of digital media. In chapter 6, these observations will be further discussed. In chapter 5, we will argue that technological characteristics of the digital media, expressed in their design, influence the process of appropriation in general and digital skills in particular. However, the most important intermediary factor is the resources people have, produced with the aid of their personal characteristics and social positions. See box 3.1.

The resources listed in box 3.1 directly influence the motivation, access, skills, and usage of digital media. For example, young people's superior medium-related digital skills may be caused by their temporal resources (having the time to experiment), social resources (a friendship network), cultural resources (enjoyment in creating these skills), and mental resources (developing abilities and intelligence while growing up in a digital media environment). This is less true for young people in developing countries, where they often lack the material resources to gain access to and learn the digital media.

The process of appropriation in terms of motivation, access, skills, and usage is also affected by the technological characteristics of the digital media concerned. It makes a big difference whether a particular medium is expensive and difficult to use or not. A tablet computer may be both cheaper and easier to use than a desktop computer with an extended keyboard and complicated software.

Box 3.1   Resources People Have

- Temporal resources: Having the time to use and reach experience with digital media;
- Material resources: Possessions and income;
- Mental resources: Technical ability and intelligence;
- Social resources: Having a social network or environment that assists with access and use;
- Cultural resources: The enjoyment and the status of using digital media.

Characteristics
of ICTs

| Personal and positional categorical inequalities | Distribution of resources | Access to ICTs | Participation in society |

Figure 3.1   A Causal Model of Resources and Appropriation Theory.
Source: Van Dijk, 2005, p. 15.

The main effects of differential appropriation of digital media are more or less participation in several fields of society. This is the core argument in this chapter. This is why digital skills, as a crucial aspect in the total process of appropriation, are the key to the information society. In the following section, the fields and types of participation will be extensively discussed.

More or less participation feeds back on existing personal and positional inequalities and builds more or less new resources. In this way, inequalities in the total process of appropriation of new technologies, including inequalities of skill, reinforce existing forms of social inequalities. The complete argument is portrayed in figure 3.1. Note that the box "Access to ICTs" must be filled with the four types of access drawn in figure 1.1.

The Stakes: More or Less Participation in Society

Growing digital media use enables more and better participation in contemporary society in several fields. In his book *The Deepening Divide*, one of the authors of the current book argued that the main stakes of having access to and skills for digital media were economic, educational, political, social, cultural, and institutional participation in society. Now, seven years after writing that book, this view has become even more evident. Digital media have merged into daily life. In developed countries, computer use has become less a lifestyle option; it has more and more become an everyday necessity (Castells, 2002). Living without computers is becoming increasingly difficult, as one would miss a growing number of opportunities. On several occasions, people will even be excluded from vital resources. We will provide a short indication for a number of fields.

Economic Participation

Every job seeker knows that the ability to work with computers and the Internet is crucial to find and obtain a job and, increasingly, to complete a job. The number of jobs that do not require digital skills is quickly declining. Locating jobs increasingly requires the use of job vacancy sites and electronic applications. In job interviews, employers ever more request certificates or other proofs of digital skills. Economists and educational scientists have calculated that having training and job experience in ICT yields a skill premium for wages (Dimaggio & Bonikowski, 2008; Goldin & Katz, 2008; Goss & Phillips, 2002; Kim, 2003; Mossberger, Johns, & King, 2006; Nahuis & De Groot, 2003). A part of the growing income inequality in the United States since the 1970s is accounted for by unequally divided ICT skills in jobs (Goldin & Katz, 2008).

In our annual Trend Surveys of Internet use in the Netherlands,[1] we presented the following statement, "After an online application considering a vacancy, I have obtained a job." This was affirmed by 18 percent of the Dutch population in 2013. The analysis showed that correlations with the level of operational, communication, and strategic skills, as measured by self-assessment questions, were highly significant. The opportunities on a job and the skill premium in earnings are caused by both the presumed higher productivity of skilled Internet users and the improved access to information. They are also created by "faster and more efficient communication, greater access to learning opportunities, or higher job satisfaction leading to greater job commitment" (Dimaggio & Bonikowski, 2008, p. 231). People with high-level communication skills are able to use their social capital or relationships for opportunity hoarding, for example, important contacts inform them about the availability of a particular job. Communication skills are also important in impressing employers, as they signal that someone who has experience in using computers and the Internet is a qualified and productive worker (Dimaggio & Bonikowski, 2008, p. 229).

Economic participation is not only a matter of finding jobs, it also involves participating in a market economy and obtaining benefits in terms of prices and profits. In our 2013 survey, we presented respondents the following statement: "By means of the Internet, I was able to buy a product cheaper than in a shop." This was confirmed by 75 percent of the Dutch population. Positive answers appeared to be mainly supported by strategic skills, with operational skills rated second. Obtaining price benefits is a matter of smart decision-making with the aid of price comparison sites and operational skills such as the quick use of toolbars, buttons, and menus.

Exchanging products on the web was part of the following statement: "By means of the Internet, I was able to sell or exchange something I otherwise would not have lost." This was affirmed by 66 percent in 2012 and 68 percent in 2013. Here, formal, communication and strategic skills were most significant. Dealing and bargaining require not only fast navigation and browsing across many offers on different sites and choice menus in online auctions and market places but also high-level communication and decision-making skills. Finally, the statement, "By means of the Internet, I have ever reached a discount on a product," was affirmed by 39 percent. This result mainly required communication and strategic skills.

Educational Participation

Today, all schools in developed countries, at all levels of education, include the use of computers and the Internet in their curricula. Here, attending school is equivalent to using these media and being able to operate them. In the primary education of rich countries, children largely learn to use computers and the Internet at home before they enter school. At school, they receive additional instruction and a focus on using these digital media for learning, not only for entertainment. In chapter 6, we will argue that the emphasis in primary and secondary education is on operational and formal skills and that information skills such as the appropriate use of search engines are often neglected. Communication skills for the Internet are not taught, except in a few marginal classes of media education. The same is true for strategic skills. When these skills are learned, they are applied to curriculum goals such as completing assignments and preparing for exams.

Thus, in developed countries, operational and formal skills are required to follow education at every level, both initial and adult education. It is impossible to complete school without these skills. Yet, higher, content-related Internet skills are equally important for educational participation and economic participation. In fact, education prepares one for a successful economic career. Information and strategic skills are required to find and follow a course of adult education on the Internet. In our annual 2013 Internet survey, 14 percent supported the statement, "Thanks to the Internet, I was able to find a course or training that suited the time, place and contents I preferred." People with sufficient strategic kills were significantly more able to accomplish this task.

Political Participation

A third domain is the growing use of digital media in political communication. The Internet brings many opportunities for increased and improved political information retrieval. It also offers many new venues for political discussion such as online forums, chatboxes, weblogs, Twitter, and other social media. Finally, it has produced new tools that support political decision-making such as voting guides and online polls, referenda, elections, and petitions.

However, contrary to popular expectations in the 1990s, the Internet is not drawing more people into the political process (Bimber, 2003; Brundidge & Rice, 2009; Katz & Rice, 2002; Quan-Haase, Wellman, Witte, & Hampton, 2002; Scheufele & Nisbet, 2002). The first evident reason is that new technical opportunities do not fix basic problems of a lack of political motivation. A second reason might be a lack of digital skills. Online discussion channels and decision-making tools require a high level of information, communication, strategic, and content creation skills. As we attempt to show in this book, these skills are unequally divided among people with high and low levels of education. In our 2013 annual survey, 31 percent of the highly educated Dutch participated in politics or discussions on government policy compared to 18 percent of the less educated. Without adequate digital skills among the mass of the population, the Internet will only increase the inequality of political participation.

The potential of the Internet for political participation is evident. In the 2013 survey, 30 percent of the Dutch affirmed the statement, "By means of the Internet, I have discovered which political party I would like to vote for." Not surprisingly, strategic skills provided the most support for this statement. The high percentage is mainly due to the popular use of electronic voting guides in the Netherlands.

Social Participation

Now, we turn to the social domain. The use of computers and the Internet is able to increase so-called social capital in terms of social contact, civic engagement, and sense of community (Katz & Rice, 2002; Quan-Haase et al., 2002). According to the research projects compiled in Wellman and Haythornthwaite (2002) and Katz and Rice (2002), the effects of Internet use on social capital are either neutral or positive. "The Internet complements and even strengthens offline interactions, provides frequent uses for social interaction and extends communication with family and friends" (Katz & Rice, 2002, p. 326).

Clearly, the Internet adds new forms of social capital to the traditional forms (e.g., dinner parties, sporting games, club house meetings, and local bars or dancing locations). The main vehicles for these new forms are social media or social networking sites, which have recently increased in popularity. Valkenburg, Peter, and Schouten (2006) found that using social networking sites increased the frequency of interaction with friends, which, in turn, resulted in positive effects on self-esteem and satisfaction with life. In our 2012 and 2013 annual surveys, 33 percent and 34 percent respectively confirmed the statement, "By means of the Internet, I have acquired one or more friends that I have met later in real life." Social participation in communities was also supported by Internet use. The statement, "By means of the Internet, I have run into an association I became a member of (such as a sports club, a cultural association, a trade union or a political organization)" was supported by 12 percent in 2013.

These positive effects do not exist for all individuals in the same ways and to the same extent. Although social media are increasingly popular among large sections of the population, their usage frequency currently is highest among young people and the reasonably educated. A minimum level of operational and formal skills is needed to begin communicating in these media. Not surprisingly, communication skills were the main competencies in finding new friends on the Internet. Becoming a member of an association was most highly correlated with communication and strategic skills, followed by the formal skills needed to work with the websites of associations.

In social networking, the design of an attractive and informative personal profile also primarily requires communication and strategic skills. As argued in the prior chapter, one should know how to present oneself in these profiles with textual and visual aids to attract new visitors, satisfy existing contacts, and convince other people.

This is especially true for online dating. In our 2013 survey, 13 percent of the Dutch Internet population at large (including very young and very old people) affirmed the statement, "Via a dating site, I have made an appointment with a potential partner." To be successful in finding a date, one must be able to select suitable candidates from an extended list (information skills). In addition, one must devise a profile that is both attractive and repulsive (for those not wanted), which requires advanced communication skills. Finally, one should be able to find a date, which includes convincing a candidate to communicate and eventually to meet. This belongs to the strategic Internet skills. In our survey, communication skills appeared to be the most significant background of online dating.

Cultural Participation

In the cultural domain, a substantial and diverse supply of leisure- and entertainment-related content has arisen since the advent of the World Wide Web. The main applications are playing games, listening to and sharing music, watching videos, using forms for collectively practicing hobbies, and sharing and trading cultural objects such as pictures, stories, and drawings. Overall, many leisure and cultural organizations are present on the Internet. One of the most prominent leisure activities can be found in the tourism domain. Planning and booking holidays on the Internet is becoming a worldwide trend. This has become the most important industry in electronic commerce. In our 2013 survey, 63 percent of Dutch Internet users confirmed the statement, "Via the Internet, I have booked a profitable holiday trip." Those who confirmed this statement appeared to have significantly more information, communication, and strategic skills.

Much of the leisure and entertainment supply is preprogrammed for a large market of consumers and relatively easy to use. However, a minimum level of operational and formal skills is needed for consumption. Contributing to so-called user-generated content in peer-to-peer networking in the cultural and entertainment domain requires additional skills. Content creation skills enable the production of culture in everyday life, making the individual creator more satisfied by giving them a project they can share with others (Gauntlett, 2011).

Spatial Participation

Spatial participation indicates that one is able to visit more geographical locations in society by leading a mobile life. This requires the use of schedules and calendars that fine-tune times and places. Visiting many different places is informative and continually allows new opportunities. The digital media offer important tools in this respect. The ability to use these tools also allows people more chances to be effective and efficient in daily life, both at work and in leisure time. In our 2013 Internet usage trend survey, 24 percent of Dutch users affirmed the statement, "By means of the Internet, I have become more flexible in my work." Seventy-one percent supported the statement, "By means of the Internet, I have become better reachable for others." People with lower levels of education were less likely to support these statements, whereas those with higher levels of education were more likely to affirm them.

However, people from lower social classes lead a much steadier and locally bound life than people from higher social classes (Castells, 1998; Van Dijk, 2005). They perform local and primarily manual work and are fixed to particular locations, whereas those individuals in higher social classes have intellectual jobs with more spatial mobility and long-distance network connections that offer career opportunities. In the trend survey mentioned above, people who affirmed the statements about flexibility and communication anytime and anyplace possessed significantly more formal, information, and strategic skills.

Institutional Participation

The last type of participation is vital in the most literal sense. Healthcare participation is rarely voluntary, as it can be a matter of life and death. Similarly, the reception of public and government services such as social and economic benefits can be a crucial means for sustaining life. Public institutions in the high-access countries often seem to believe that they can reach the entire population with online public and health services. Some even believe that they will be able to close the traditional channels of service provision in the near future. Unfortunately, this is a big mistake, as a large portion of the population in these countries does not use the Internet or does not use it for public services (e.g., International Telecommunications Union, 2013).Those who use them, often have difficulties in finding the information needed, completing forms, and realizing online transactions (Van Deursen & Pieterson, 2006; Van Deursen, Van Dijk, & Ebbers, 2006).

Individuals who are not able to realize these online activities receive fewer public, social, and financial (e.g., tax) benefits. Increasingly, those who only utilize service desks and the telephone are less informed and slower in receiving benefits and other provisions for citizens.

The most vital domain of institutional Internet use and participation in sectors of society is health. The use of the Internet for health services is rapidly growing and has become a popular application. An increasing number of websites directly address people by providing information about health problems, self-care, and prevention. Uses of these sites include searching for health information, Internet-based peer support groups, online health consultations, and the delivery of health interventions (Griffiths, Lindenmeyer, Powell, Lowe, & Thorogood, 2006). The possible benefits are immediate, complete, and convenient access to health information when people believe that they have a health problem. Further, people can receive anonymous help when feeling embarrassed or stigmatized. Patients can have information control over a particular medical advice or a treatment that is running and they can support each other in online support groups. Finally, they can retrieve additional information next to that of their doctors.

However, unfortunately, people who have the most frequent health problems and the highest mortality rates, that is, people with low education and the elderly, have the least access to and skills in using these opportunities. This problem occurs, for example, when the unskilled cannot find the hospital with the shortest waiting list for surgery or doctors with the best qualifications. This also occurs when they lack other crucial information that helps them in preventing or relieving an urgent disease or when they are not able ask for a second opinion about a proposed treatment.

Digital skills are especially important in the health field because medical information is rather complex, specialist, and difficult to find. This is true for both online and offline health media, but digital applications do not simplify the matter. These applications can increase the difficulty in retrieving the information needed. Many health websites tend to present all available information in technical and specialist terms to a population that is unfamiliar with them. They offer few tools to help people find relevant information in the excessive amounts that they provide (Benigeri & Pluye, 2003). A second problem is that most people cannot evaluate the quality of online health information (Pandolfini, Impicciatore, & Bonati, 2000; Shepperd, Charnock, & Gann, 1999). A final problem is that many patients are not able to understand the information retrieved and put it into practice (D'Alessandro, Kingsley, & Johnson-West, 2001). Thus, a mixture of media-related and content-related digital skills is required for effective online health communication.

In our 2013 annual Internet survey, 16 percent of users affirmed the statement, "By means of the Internet, I have discovered which medical illness I had." Adequate strategic skills that enabled them to choose the correct illness were the most important competencies of those who provided a positive answer. The second aid in finding and evaluating health information was information and communication skills. The third type of skills commanded by those who were able to find the disease was operational skills. This result can be explained by the many elderly who need health information but perform relatively poorly in operational skills.

From this short overview of participation in important domains of society, we can gather that the stakes of not having access to the digital media and not being able to work with them are high. The answers to the statements we proposed demonstrate that the ability to use the Internet, as the most important current digital medium, and having the skills required are critical. Even in this relatively early stage of the evolution of the Internet, the ability to use it creates real benefits. Soon, individuals' levels of Internet skills will be associated with inclusion or exclusion from society.

What Is the Problem with a Lack of Digital Media Skills?

Exclusion from society is a serious problem. Yet, some people attempt to downplay it. They have three apparently strong arguments. The first is that for all practical goals and every type of participation in society, traditional media remain available. The second is that the social inequality observed in digital media skills and usage is nothing new. Throughout history, there have been inequalities in media use. Literate, intelligent, and powerful people have always been the first and the best in utilizing media. The last argument is that those with a lack of digital skills often have someone around them helping out (or even taking over) when performing a task that requires the use of digital media. Let us closely consider these three arguments.

In virtually all sections of society, age-old channels of communication continue to be used, sometimes even more often than digital media. Specially in developing countries, traditional media are still frequently used. Well-known alternatives are the traditional telephone, print media and writing, and service desks assisted by the most important medium, face-to-face communication. Most organizations, particularly public and government organizations, adopt so-called multichannel strategies that offer a choice of telephone, printed form, Internet, email, and service-desk delivery. In the first stages of Internet diffusion, many organizations dreamed about full online service delivery because it was cheaper, faster, and more efficient. Banks, for instance, closed one branch after another. After some time, they altered their strategy because online-only provision did not appear to work well with complex products and services. Such products and services required human assistance and high-level communication with customers and clients. Today, multichannel strategies with a mixture of traditional and digital media are dominant in consumer markets and public services. However, slowly but surely, the share of digital media is increasing.

The argument that traditional media remain available for many goals or functions in society is correct, but it becomes weaker by the day. In countries with high levels of Internet access, businesses and even governments are tempted to offer only online services and close service desks and call-centers. For example, the Dutch Tax and Custom Service is considering accepting only electronic tax forms from citizens. Since 2005, Dutch businesses have experienced obligatory electronic tax filing. In an increasing number of high-access countries, tickets for concerts and other cultural events can only be purchased electronically. With a more than 80 percent Internet access rate, an increasing number of businesses and public organizations are likely to close traditional channels. They make the case that the few not having access to the Internet can use the help and facilities of family members or neighbors or go to public access sites.

Obligatory online access and use is not the only argument against the availability of traditional media as a remaining option. The second case is that digital media offer a number of opportunities that are absent in the traditional media. After all, digital media have been created for practical reasons. To provide a few examples, price comparison sites afford faster and more accurate comparisons than visiting a number of shops in a mall. Furthermore, searching for a particular disease on a health information site is better focused, more up-to-date and specific than a printed brochure or medical encyclopedia. Additionally, it is possible to send an email with questions to a doctor. Maintaining and expanding one's social network on a daily basis with a social network site is easier, better informed, and up-to-date than calling or meeting friends at public locations. Determining which political party to vote for is easier and more systematic in an online voting guide that enables a choice for or against particular statements than assembling and comparing a number of printed political programs or extensively viewing political broadcasting that might be one-sided. People with insufficient access and skills simply miss these attractive opportunities. These opportunities are steadily growing with the stream of new applications offered on the web and smart mobile telephony.

The second argument against the claim that the inequalities of digital skills are a special problem is that it is nothing new. Inequalities of literacy and knowledge are age-old, at least since the invention of writing. Two claims are made. The first claim is that traditional and digital media literacies have more similarities than differences. The second is that both traditional and digital media inequality affect the social categories in the same way. The less educated, the poor, the elderly, and the differently abled perform relatively poorly on all skills. These claims are only partially correct.

The first claim is correct when it refers to particular new media experts who have made the mistake of regarding digital skills as special and completely different from the skills needed in traditional media. A first look at the list of traditional and digital media skills in boxes 1.1 and 1.2 reveals that there is considerable similarity and overlap. However, the claim also tends to downplay the basic differences between traditional and digital media skills. Concerning traditional media skills, inequalities of literacy, knowledge, and mental activity are emphasized. Digital media require additional skills. In addition to these (and other) mental competencies, they require user activity. Computer and Internet users must interact with interfaces. A minimum level of active engagement with the medium is required. The Internet offers the possibility of interaction, transaction, and interpersonal communication.

The Internet is characterized by extended multi-functionality (Van Dijk & Hacker, 2003). To use this functionality, Internet users must learn the higher content-related digital skills. These skills include consuming and creating content, communicating through interactivity rather than one-sided sending and receiving, and making decisions to continually act rather than passively consume media content and incidentally create content. The Internet offers dozens of types of applications for various types of communication and media use and for all domains of human life. These applications touch every aspect of daily life and are used at work, school, home, and in transit. The range of skills required to fully use these applications is broad; thus, inequalities in commanding them amplify all other existing inequalities. Therefore, the societal impact of the inequality of digital skills is much larger than that of traditional media skills.

The societal impact of this inequality is demonstrated in the observation of a usage gap concerning Internet applications that is comparable to the knowledge gap suggested in the 1970s concerning traditional mass media. Tichenor, Donohue, and Olien (1970) claimed that when the infusion of mass media information into a social system increases, segments of the population with higher socioeconomic statuses tend to acquire this information at a faster rate than the lower-status segments. In short, people with higher education and status would learn more from television, radio, newspapers, and other mass media than people with lower education and status.

While the knowledge gap refers to the differential derivation of *knowledge* from the mass media, the usage gap is a broader thesis that potentially reaches further and is more relevant for society. It refers to differential *uses and activities* in all spheres of daily life, not only the perception and cognition of mass media. The usage gap thesis claims that people with better social positions and higher education use significantly more so-called serious Internet applications that aid them in their work, careers, business, and studies, whereas people with the lesser positions and lower education use more applications for entertainment, simple communication, and shopping. Several survey researchers have found evidence for such a gap (e.g., Bonfadelli, 2002; Bunz, 2009; Howard, Rainie, & Jones, 2001; Madden, 2003; Van Deursen & Van Dijk, 2014a; Van Dijk, 1999; Van Dijk & Hacker, 2003; Zillien & Hargittai, 2009).

Behind the concept and thesis of a usage gap, a clear normative account comes forward. The assumption is that several Internet usage activities are more beneficial or advantageous for Internet users than other activities are. Some activities offer users more chances and resources to move forward in their career, work, education, and societal position than other activities that are mainly consumptive or entertaining.

The background of this usage gap lies in a combination of technological and social, cultural, or personal characteristics. Technological characteristics are the complexity, expensiveness, and multi-functionality of computer and Internet technology, which invite different uses (Van Dijk, 2005). Personal characteristics are varied motivations to use the Internet and other digital media. They range from information seeking, education and career development to online shopping, online gaming, and other online entertainment. Social characteristics are positions occupied. Individuals with a high-level job or course of study are stimulated to use more serious applications, whereas those with a low-level job or who are unemployed are less motivated to use these serious applications. Parents of school-aged children are motivated to engage with the educational programs that their children practice in their homework. Cultural backgrounds are the differentiation and individualization of (post)modern society, leading to an increasing number of diverging interests. However, differences in digital skills are another cause of the usage gap. In particular, the lack of content-related skills such as information and strategic skills prevents Internet users from choosing complex and serious applications.

The second claim announced above is that traditional and digital media inequalities touch social categories in the same way. This claim is only partially correct. Educational background seems equally related to differences in traditional and digital media skills. However, the need to learn to use digital technology creates an extra barrier that appears to be greater for the less educated than for the highly educated. In terms of gender, there is scarcely any difference between the skills of males and females in using traditional and digital media in developed countries, where the emancipation of women occurred in the twentieth century. However, in less developed countries, often with cultures of male domination, digital technology erects an extra barrier. When these technologies are scarce, they are reserved for males. The clearest differences in terms of skills among social categories are related to age. Seniors are strikingly behind in medium-related digital skills compared to younger people, especially the so-called digital natives. In contrast, the opposite is true for traditional skills. With advancing age, people increase their traditional literacy skills until they reach the years of decaying vision and mental ability.

The third argument of those trying to downplay the importance of digital skills insufficiencies that we will reveal in the next chapter, is that people with a lack of digital skills often have assistance by closed ones. Family members, friends, neighbors, or acquaintances with some level of digital skills are supposed to be available for almost everyone. Although having a social network is very important for acquiring digital skills, we think this argument is not convincing. It sounds fairly similar to the popular nineteenth-century view that a letter received by an illiterate father could as well be read by his son without having the need to learn to read himself. In the twenty-first century every individual of a particular age needs basic level of digital skills or literacy to perform in society. This is the main message of this book. At present, digital skills are becoming part of compulsory education in most countries while older citizens have to learn these skills in adult education.

In addition to this normative counterargument, it is very likely that people with lower levels of digital skills, also have relatively less people in their vicinity with sufficient levels of digital skills than people who already possess adequate levels of skills. Sociologists often observed that people living in poor neighborhoods and low class or status environments have relatively small social networks and have little opportunity to ask for effective assistance (Tilly, 1998). This also applies for those having a problem with having access to and use of digital media (Witte & Mannon, 2010). In their environment, assistance will be poor and not immediately available, which results in losing time and opportunities in using digital media. This state of affairs reflects social inequality in general.

Unequal Digital Skills: A Reflection of Social Inequality in General

We cannot conclude that all remains the same with the transition from traditional to digital media skills. Yet, continuity is stronger than change. The same types of social and information inequalities appear in digital media skills and traditional media skills. The main difference is technology, more precisely, *the use* of technology in particular social practices, or the tools that are used in the appropriation of digital media. This creates a number of additional barriers for those who experience problems in using digital technology and grants new opportunities for those who skillfully operate this technology. As we will see in the next chapter, operational, formal, and content creation skills are the main obstacle for seniors; however, the information and strategic skills that they learned in the traditional media might prevail when this obstacle is removed. For people with low education, the technical medium-related operational and formal skills required often raise an additional barrier. For these individuals, removing this barrier does not give way to information and strategic skills because they lack a high level of these skills. For differently abled and illiterate individuals, the difficulty and novelty of digital technologies are an additional handicap, although they also may provide solutions such as zoom functions on screens for the visually handicapped and multimedia pictures surrounding text for illiterates. In chapter 6, we will discuss these barriers and opportunities for differently abled and illiterate media users.

With the exception of the role of technology, inequalities in digital skills are a reflection of social and information inequality in general. This statement is consistent with the model of Resources and Appropriation Theory portrayed in figure 3.1. According to this model, ICT access (digital skills are the third phase of ICT access) is caused by both characteristics of ICTs and existing personal and positional inequalities that lead to the possession of different resources. These inequalities and the resources that they produce are what we consider as a reflection of existing social and information inequality. The model shows that the differences of access that they produce tend to reinforce the inequalities of participation in society and that this effect feeds back on greater inequalities between persons, positions, and resources. For example, when people have a job that contains daily work with computers and the Internet, they will most likely develop more digital skills than those without such a job. This work will increase their career opportunities (economic participation) and provide them new positions (better jobs), new personal characteristics ("technical intelligence"), and new resources (higher wages, more time to spend on digital media, technical competencies, experience with cyber-culture, and more social contacts via the web).

These effects of reinforcement are explained in network theory. In his book *The Network Society*, one of the authors of the current book has described a number of so-called "laws of the web." One of these "laws" is the law of trend amplification. It is summarized as follows: "Networks are relational structures that tend to amplify existing social and structural trends. When technologies such as ICT networks and computers are used, they serve as reinforcing tools." (Van Dijk, 2012, p. 42). Commanding digital skills certainly offers tools. When Internet skills are concerned, it does so in the context of a network. Digital skills strengthen one's relative position in a network, for instance, on the labor market when applying for a better job online. They help those in a better social position and those with socially higher qualified personal characteristics more than those with worse positions and qualifications.

This finding brings us to one of the most important arguments of this book. At first sight, it seems that improving people's digital skills will always help the advantaged more than the disadvantaged, increasing the relative inequality between people. Unfortunately, this is true, but only with a number of important qualifications. These qualifications inspire a feasible and realistic policy of skills improvement, which will be the core subject of the second part of this book.

The first qualification is that the improvement of digital skills has a bottom line and an upper limit. The bottom line is the command of digital skills to such an extent that one is able to gain access to and use digital media that are required to function in the information society. The minimum condition for this purpose is an adequate level of operational and formal skills. In this way, one obtains the key and is able to open the door to the information society. Subsequently, the content-related skills are needed to function more or less in this society. Typically, they are a reflection of the level of education people previously achieved. The upper limit of the improvement of digital skills appears when the most skilled users are not able to follow computer and Internet training or classes anymore, or when they are no longer prepared to listen to tips for improvement because they have command over these skills or because they believe that they do. The difference between this upper and lower limit offers a space for skills improvement that motivates those in greatest need to participate in educational solutions.

The second qualification is that those in the worst social positions and with the lowest personal qualifications can be placed in a better position and supported in personal development. The "law" of trend amplification is not a natural law but a social "law" that is liable to change. The social and personal conditions of people who must increase their digital skills can be improved by economic, social, and cultural policies. Thus, a narrowly defined digital skills improvement only partially works. We will provide two examples. First, it might be better to provide an unemployed individual a job with computer work than to provide this person a computer class only. Second, in the Third World, it might be better to provide individuals permanent access to the Internet in a community access center than to provide a onetime course in digital skills without opportunities for practice. The material, social, and personal conditions for digital skills improvement are more important than the improvement in its own right.

The prime conclusion is that digital skills improvement is able to mitigate social and information inequality despite the reinforcement effects described. However, more measures are needed than digital skills improvement only. Particular conditions for improvement have to be provided. In the final chapter of this book, we will discuss potential policy measures for governments, businesses, citizens, and their organizations to improve the economic, social, and cultural conditions of digital technology use for all.

However, in chapters 5 and 6, we will give full attention to the two most important and popular types of solutions for the inequality of digital skills that will be presented in the next chapter. The first type is improvement of technical design, the topic of the following chapter. Improving the accessibility, usability, and comprehensibility of digital media might be the most important way to prevent problems of digital skills. Better accessibility and usability of digital media will certainly reduce the demands posed on the command of operational and formal skills. Perhaps the replacement of PCs with easily accessible tablet computers will solve many known operational and formal skills problems. Improving the comprehensibility of digital media content will surely assist all content-related digital skills.

When prevention does not work sufficiently, the problem can only be repaired by helping people to use the digital media that are offered to them. This second type of solution is the most obvious solution in public opinion. It consists of various educational solutions in formal and informal education, primary and adult education, and courses and training at work or public access sites. All of these types of education and their target groups of learners will be discussed in chapter 6.

Before discussing the solutions of digital skills insufficiencies, we have to estimate the levels of all six skills as presented in our framework. In the next chapter, digital skill level estimates are derived from available evidence.

Conclusions

In this chapter, we discussed the social backgrounds and consequences of digital skills inequalities. Following Resources and Appropriation Theory, it was argued that people with unequal temporal, material, mental, social, and cultural resources appropriate more or less access to digital media, including the mastery of digital skills. The consequences of unequal access and varying digital skills mean more or less participation in all fields of society; these skills are the key to improving opportunities in life. Having sufficient levels of digital skills creates several types of potential benefits, including having and maintaining a job, higher salary, improved medical treatment, more social relationships and memberships in organizations, increased voting or other political activities, prioritized tickets for cultural performances, and even citizen benefits provided by the government. In this way, resources are distributed among people with higher or lower levels of digital skills. Thus a feedback loop occurs: these participation opportunities increase the resources people owned before (Figure 3.1).

Some people downplay the problem of digital skills inequality, claiming that traditional media still serve all needs. They claim that inequality of media use is nothing new as it occurred with all media throughout history. Furthermore, they claim that those with inadequate levels of digital skills are usually supported by individuals near them who have adequate levels of digital skills. These arguments were rejected in this chapter. Traditional media are increasingly inferior to digital media in a growing number of practices in society. Despite some similarities to traditional media skills, digital skills are also different. Digital skills require the mastery of particular relatively complex operations, interfaces, and applications of digital technology. Additionally, those with poor levels of digital skills usually have less access to assistance.

Despite the differences between traditional and digital skills, both skills are reflected by social inequality in general. As we will see in the next chapter, groups of people in society that are deprived of material, social, mental, and cultural resources also have lower levels of digital resources and skills. The only (presumably temporary) exception is the level of the medium-related digital skills of seniors. However, in the last part of the chapter, it is also argued that the use of digital technology is able to reinforce existing general social inequality. One of the reasons underlying this argument is that the digital media of networks and computers are reinforcing tools that generate results in all types of societal activities. Those who possess and are able to operate these tools benefit more than those who do not have these tools. Simultaneously, people with a strong position in social, economic, political, and cultural networks in the network society strengthen this position by commanding relatively high levels of digital skills.

Further Reading

- Van Dijk, J. A. G. M. (2005). *The deepening divide, inequality in the information society*. London; Thousand Oaks, CA; New Delhi: Sage.
  This book unfolds the Resources Appropriation Theory that backs this chapter and the digital divide in general.
- Tilly, C. (1998). *Durable inequality*. Berkeley, CA; Los Angeles, CA: University of California Press.
  A general theory of social inequality that argues that inequality is durable or reinforced in relations of power between people, especially in networks. Inequality is considered a relational characteristic between opposed category pairs such as management and employees, not an individual attribute of people such as poor or rich.
- Warschauer, M. (2003). *Technology and social inclusion: Rethinking the digital divide*. Cambridge, MA; London: The MIT Press. Also departs from a resources basis for the digital divide and digital skills. Focussed predominantly on the situation of the developing countries.
- Witte, J. C., & Mannon, S. E. (2010). *The Internet and social inequalities*. New York; London: Routledge.
  Explains the digital divide and digital skills in several sociological perspectives (conflict, cultural, and functionalist). Provides American data.
- Helsper, E. J. (2012). A corresponding fields model of digital inclusion. *Communication Theory, 22*, 403–426.
  This article proposes a theoretical model that hypothesizes how specific areas of digital and social exclusion influence each other. In this

corresponding fields model, it is argued that they relate mostly for similar (economic, cultural, social, personal) fields of resources.

- Van Deursen, A. J. A. M., & Van Dijk, J. A. G. M. (2014a). The digital divide shifts to differences in usage. *New Media & Society, 16(3)*, 507–526.
  An article that reports participation data and the thesis of the usage gap.

Note

1. Research reports (in Dutch) from 2009 to 2012 are available on www.alexander-vandeursen.nl.

CHAPTER 4

Current Levels of Internet Skills

Introduction

In chapter 2, we elaborated six types of Internet skills that the general Internet user needs to participate in an online environment. These skills are important because an increasing number of organizations in society are moving their services online and expect that all of their consumers, citizens, workers, and students have sufficient skills to use them. Unfortunately, this assumption is often unfounded. In fact, an insufficient level of Internet skills makes these services unavailable, especially when they are offered as an alternative to traditional offline services. In this chapter, we gather and present empirical evidence on the levels of command that the general Internet user population currently hold concerning the six types of Internet skills. The goal is to identify potential bottlenecks in these skills in order to define specific policies to cope with the shortcomings observed.

Unfortunately, determining the current levels of Internet skills is not simple. Although numerous scientific and nonscientific papers, books, and articles concerning literacies in the digital era exist, the empirical evidence or measurements considering populations at large is relatively scarce. Often, studies are conducted in the fields of library research, computer science, or educational science. These studies offer evidence of task performances on the individual and group level in computer classes. They collect marks and figures that are limited to the norms of the education program concerned, for example, whether the marks for a particular module of a computer driver's license exam are sufficient to pass the exam. These studies aid in understanding the level of certain skills among people in specific settings. Unfortunately, figures of the population at large and the demographic correlates are far less considered.

The lack of empirical evidence regarding the command of digital skills among entire populations is also caused by limitations in measurements. Most of the conducted studies rely on indirect measures and self-assessments in surveys. For example, in the EU Eurostat surveys, skills are indirectly measured by asking respondents how many of six Internet applications they have ever used. In this case, applications 1 and 2 correspond with lower skill levels, applications 3 and 4 correspond with intermediate levels, and applications 5 and 6 correspond with higher skill levels. In our model presented in figure 1.1, these are measurements of usage rather than skills.

Most researchers agree that respondent self-assessments are not valid measurements of the skills possessed. It is well-known that people have difficulties in judging their skills because interpretations of skills are perspective and context dependent. These interpretations depend upon, among other things, an individual's comparison group (Talja, 2005). The results of our tests revealed that content-related skills such as information seeking tend to be over-evaluated. Another question is the users' norm, that is, when are they satisfied with their performance? As users regularly achieve their practical goals, they believe that they perform well. However, the result of a search engine operation, for example, might be satisfactory according to the norm of the user but not according to an external observer who notices that superior potential search results are missed or ignored. Thus, the use of survey instruments to measure Internet skills has significant problems of validity. These instruments have proven to be a poor predictor of performance.

Observational studies are the most valid method for obtaining a realistic view of people's Internet skills. However, the cost of such studies is a strong limitation for large-scale data gathering. Hargittai (2002) conducted a series of experimental tests with American user groups charged with tasks of locating information on the Internet. Inspired by her work, the authors of the current book conducted comparable investigations with performance tests of operational, formal, information, and strategic Internet skills in a media lab in the Netherlands. Subjects were asked to complete assignments on the Internet. In a series of three studies—with a focus on governmental, general leisure, and health-related assignments—a diverse group of over three hundred Internet users was subjected to performance tests to determine their skill levels (for a detailed description of the tests, see Van Deursen, 2010, 2012; Van Deursen & Van Dijk, 2009a, 2009b, 2010, 2011a, 2011b; Van Deursen, Van Dijk, & Peters, 2011). Subjects were recruited by applying a randomly stratified sample using gender, age, and education quotas. All subjects indicated that they had prior Internet experience. Of note, the Netherlands is a country with a very high degree of broadband adoption; 97 percent of the inhabitants have broadband household access to the

Internet (Eurostat Statistics, 2013). In this book, we will use the results of these performance tests and other studies to estimate current levels of each of the six Internet skills.

We will not only focus on the levels of the six types of Internet skills but also on which segments of the general population require skill improvements. Some surprising observations will be presented. For example, we will show that popular assumptions concerning the generation of digital natives, namely, that young people who are completely immersed in digital technology are "fluent in the digital language of computers, video games and the Internet" (Prensky, 2005b, p. 8), requires serious reconsideration.

Levels of Operational Internet Skills

Based on performance tests, Hargittai (2002) concluded more than ten years ago that the general American user population lacks an understanding of the basics of surfing the Internet. In our more recent performance tests, we focused on the operational skills to use an Internet browser. We found that the general levels of operational skills among the Dutch population are quite high; covering all tests subjects completed around 75 percent of the operational Internet skills assignments. Not surprisingly, age was an important factor in the operational assignment completion. Several studies have found age-related differences in older adults' learning and use of computers and the Internet. The difficulties older adults experience are related to age-associated changes in visual, perceptual, psychomotor, and cognitive abilities (Xie, 2003). For instance, a number of studies suggest that age-related changes in psychomotor abilities affect older adults' use of computer input devices such as the mouse and the keyboard, while impaired eyesight affects older adults' use of computers and the Internet. Chapter 6 will go deeper into age-related changes of the elderly.

The first operational skill set defined in the prior chapter concerns the use of toolbars, buttons, and menu's in all kinds of Internet services. In our performance tests, we tested these skills when using an Internet browser. The use of an Internet browser is not straightforward for seniors. Some of them did not even recognize the browser if Google was not displayed. They did not seem to have a clue on how to proceed and seemed unfamiliar with use of the browser's address bar. In some cases, they did not recognize the address bar at all, or they found the jump from the web browser to the small URL address window a difficult transition. Some also did not remove the current URL when entering a new one, resulting in a page not found message. Others were convinced that websites could only be opened by using the

"Open" option in the browser's menu. When they opened a website, some subjects seemed to be not aware of additional information existing beyond the frame of the browser window; at least they did not scroll to preview the whole webpage. The operational skill to add a website to the bookmarks did not appear to be a problem. Although quite a lot of subjects seemed unfamiliar with this possibility, they were able to find the corresponding browser button.

The second operational skill set defined here concerns the required user input. Filling all kinds of forms with different input fields did not reveal many problems in our tests. A few subjects forgot to complete the whole form, which resulted in a warning message that caused confusion. Concerning the use of a search engine, it appeared that a few subjects overlooked the search engine on a website (while obviously present) or experienced input related problems such as typing keywords without spaces or keywords preceded by "www." A recurring mistake also identified in other studies is the use of multiple terms without any spaces between them (e.g., Birru et al., 2004; Hargittai, 2002). Some seniors entered search queries into the address bar. Other problems concerned clicking too much times on search buttons or using the right mouse button instead of the left when trying to enter text in a box.

Finally, concerning opening and saving files, we found that in our performance tests almost half of all subjects did not succeed in saving a PDF file on the desktop. These subjects did not seem to be able to distinguish between saving a file by clicking on a link to that file, and saving a website or webpage. Some people had absolutely no clue on how to proceed in the task of saving a file such as a brochure, music, or video fragment. Other mistakes included: assuming that the file was automatically saved after opening the save dialog, making website shortcuts to the desktop, or bookmarking a website instead of saving a file.

Empirical data concerning operational skills for specific Internet services are scarce. Concerning email, research suggests that most people only know a fraction of the features of email programs that in theory enable a more efficient use of this medium (Dean, 2009). Examples are the problematic use of CC and BCC, not filing incoming messages in folders, or dealing inadequately with spam, to mention just a few. Learning email mainly occurs by trial and error. However, the most disturbing fact is that many people think they can handle email as they have learned it in practice, while actually they are inefficient in using it.

In our tests, aging and lower levels of education seemed to contribute to the amount of experienced operational skill-related problems. Saving files, bookmarking websites, and the basic use of search engines were especially troublesome for seniors and people with lower levels of education. In contrast, young people seem to be familiar with most of these actions.

Levels of Formal Internet Skills

We defined formal skills as the ability to navigate hypermedia environments without becoming disorientated. People who have difficulties with navigation and orientation on the web often ascribe these problems to design and usability issues. Several studies assume a technical perspective in which the design of the website or platform is tested for navigational issues while the users' navigation and orientation skills deficiencies are neglected. Formal Internet skills are important for effectively using different online menus, browsing within and between websites and browsing search results, online discussions, emails, contact lists, among other tasks.

Similar to operational Internet skills, the general opinion is that senior populations in particular lack formal skills. There is indeed evidence that the Internet presents obstacles to users with cognitive or mobility impairments that make navigation difficult (e.g., O'Hara, 2004). Navigating a loosely organized nonlinear site can frustrate people with short-term memory impairments (Nielsen, 2002). However, although there are several studies on navigating hypermedia, these studies rarely consider demographic correlates; thus, the relationship with individual differences is unclear. This is unfortunate, as becoming lost or disoriented is one of the most significant problems in hypermedia navigation. Users can become lost due to the nonlinear nature of hypermedia systems (Chen & Macredie, 2002). If there is considerable cross-referencing among pages, looping behavior may also result (Boechler, 2001). Of note, there have been only a few attempts to assess and quantify the status of being lost, which is difficult to measure (e.g., Gwizdka & Spence, 2007; Herder, 2003).

The performance tests conducted in our media lab revealed several problems that can be ascribed to formal skill insufficiencies. We used four tasks to measure formal Internet skills. On average, 75 percent of the skills were successfully completed. Only approximately 45 percent of the respondents completed all four tasks successfully. In the first formal skill task, we attempted to identify related problems by asking respondents to find a simple piece of information (e.g., street address) on websites with very different layouts and design features. During the completion of this task, some subjects overlooked options or links in the websites' main menus, whereas others did not recognize these menus. There were also subjects who altered the URL, for example, adding "/address," believing that this would bring them directly to the requested contact details. During the tests, approximately 40 percent of the subjects experienced problems while using menus. Rollover menus were especially problematic for senior users, who did not understand why the appearing menu suddenly disappeared when (unbeknownst to them) the mouse pointer was moved outside the menu area. Hopefully, touchscreens that are now available on many devices help to overcome this problem. Recent studies among older adults provide evidence that menu selection performance by using a keyboard and mouse is less compared to touchscreens (e.g., Nic, 2009).

In the second task, we attempted to measure whether respondents were able to maintain their orientation while navigating within websites. The subjects were asked to navigate toward a page in a large website and subsequently asked to return to the homepage from a deep-link. This appeared to be a problem for 28 percent of the subjects. The subjects often believed that they were on the homepage already; they clicked "Up" rather than "Home" (while they were already at the top of a page) or clicked on a link to the current page. One subject attempted to find the homepage using the Internet browser's help function, and another attempted to call his brother by phone to ask for help in finding the homepage. Some individuals were not familiar with the fact that a small home icon or a company logo would bring them back to the homepage of the website. In fact, many users did not seem to recognize image links as if they were not labeled as a link.

In the third task, we attempted to measure problems related to orientation between websites by instructing subjects to click a link to an external website and return to the homepage of the original website. Of all subjects, 21 percent lost their orientation when a new browser window was opened. They did not understand why the back button (in the new window) was deactivated and overlooked the website in the original window, even when it remained visible in the background. Some of the participants closed all windows and started again. Similar problems occurred during the completion of larger information skill assignments in which the subjects were asked to locate information. During these tasks, some subjects were relocated to another website without noticing that this occurred. Additionally, they did not see the original window or tab after opening a new one. The same appeared to be the case when using the browser tabs. When a website was opened in a new tab, many users seemed to be unaware that the original website remained open in a prior tab.

Maintaining orientation when navigating search results was measured in the fourth task. The subjects were asked to open the first and fourth search result after performing a search operation. One-third of the subjects experienced problems with this task. The main problem was that after opening the first search result, the subjects chose the fourth option in a nearby menu that was not related to the generated search results. They were convinced that they opened the fourth search result, indicating that a website's structure causes a false orientation without the user noticing his or her mistake. Some subjects opened the fourth page with search results rather than the fourth search result. Several subjects did not return to the original search result list after opening the first search result; rather, they navigated to the homepage again, retyped the same search query and opened the fourth result.

An analysis of the performance test results revealed that age and educational level of attainment appeared to be significant contributors to both the number of successfully completed formal skill tasks and the time spent on the tasks. Most of the formal skill-related problems described above were experienced by the elderly and by people with lower levels of education. In addition, increased Internet experience led to less time being spent on the assignments. In our tests, we did not find differences in performance between men and women. However, some older studies revealed that women report higher levels of spatial anxiety, which is negatively related to the orientation required in way-finding strategies (Ford & Miller, 1996; Lawton, 1994).

The above findings are based on web navigation and orientation when using relatively large displays. When small displays on mobile devices such as smartphones or tablet PCs are used, one might expect that problems related to navigation and orientation might occur relatively more often. Although touchscreens on such devices might support navigation, the site structures and available support systems for navigation are different. To maintain one's orientation, users of small screens are forced to navigate texts and other contents backward and forward more often to provide context. They must use scrolling mechanisms to a larger degree to help them make sense of the pages visited than is the case with conventional desktop or laptop screens. Furthermore, still most websites are designed to fit conventionally sized display windows, making their use on small screens difficult and placing extra stress on the levels of formal Internet skills. Although users might become increasingly accustomed to such devices and screens, for many, much time and practice are needed before navigation and orientation on these devices proceed with ease. If these skills are not fully developed, it is difficult to perform high levels of information, communication, and strategic Internet skills on such devices. Fortunately, non-user-friendly web designs, unorganized content, and difficulty of navigation information on mobile devices such as smartphones are decreasing with the introduction of apps and page formats that are adapted or specifically designed for these devices.

Levels of Information Internet Skills

Of all the skills discussed in this book, information skills have gained the most attention in the scientific literature. Information-searching skills are especially studied in educational contexts in which students' searching strategies are investigated. There is general agreement that information skills are important in the continuously growing digital environment. The results of most studies, however, suggest that the general Internet user has limited knowledge of search engines and lacks the skills required to conduct a systematic information search session. Our performance tests confirm these findings. In all studies, 55 percent of the search assignments were completed successfully.

Other research findings demonstrate that end users do not conduct particularly sophisticated online searches, although the vast majority of users are satisfied with their findings (Markey, 2007). However, a satisfied outcome of the search task does not automatically mean that all of the defined steps in the search process are adequately addressed. In this section, we will discuss the five steps of the search process. Of note, the search assignments in our performance tests were not particularly difficult; they were applicable to the general Internet user and would be generally considered easy to solve.

Defining the Information Problem

Defining the information problem is important in obtaining a clear view of the problem (e.g., Hill, 1999; Land & Greene, 2000). However, defining the information need or search object(s), is not as simple as it sounds for general users. Few tools are available to help define the problem. Defining the information problem is characterized by feelings of uncertainty and by unclear and general thoughts. In a literature overview, Walraven, Brand-Gruwel & Boshuizen (2008) concluded that adults have less trouble with defining the information problem than teenagers. Most teenagers begin searching immediately without exploring the topic, planning the search, or thinking about the task (Duijkers, Gulikers-Dinjens & Boshuizen, 2001; Fidel et al., 1999). Walraven et al. (2008) summarized the teenagers' problems as follows: "When teenagers had to search for information on the World-Wide Web about a subject matter to accomplish a task, they had trouble with formulating useful inquiry questions. They often asked questions with a single correct answer instead of questions that required them to synthesize information from multiple sources. They asked a somewhat general question and tried to find information on it. When they could not find information to answer their question they simply changed the question. They adapted the question to available information found online and had troubles with posing good and rich questions" (p. 628).

Although not explicitly measured, the results of our performance tests suggest the same conclusion. While younger subjects immediately began the online search, older subjects tended to first think about the assignment. Note that in the performance tests, the problem definition was partially provided in the task description. Although the search tasks were relatively easy and small, during the tests, many users had difficulties with defining the search object(s). Examples of assignments include finding a restaurant with the most Michelin stars in the city of Amsterdam, determining which documents are needed when applying for a passport, and finding the name of a specific disease. As we will discuss in the next steps, the queries observed in the searches indicate that the searcher may not have well considered the search object(s). It is rare for individuals to write down exactly what he or she is looking for before starting an online search (we believe this might certainly help!).

Choosing a Search System

The most common strategies for locating information on the Internet are using search engines, entering URLs in the browser's address bar, and browsing subject categories. In our tests, most people turned to the same system for all of their information assignments, namely, Google. In the operational skill section, we indicated that some seniors even considered Google as being the Internet; without seeing Google after starting up an Internet browser, they did not know how to proceed. Turning to only one system appears to be the overall observation of numerous studies (e.g., Jansen & Pooch, 2000). The problem is that this does not always result in locating the most relevant information.

Our tests revealed that in some instances, respondents employed strategies other than using Google to locate desired information. For instance, they began with websites used in the past or by guessing URLs. Most of the time, this resulted in a trial and error strategy without any underlying systematic approach. Such strategies lack the efficiency and effectiveness necessary for quality results. One man (aged 44), for example, was asked to find the costs of a particular parking lot in the city of Rotterdam. Rather than beginning the search at the municipality website or using a search engine, he directly typed www.parkeergarage.nl (www.parkinglot.nl) into the URL. The website existed, but the content was far from relevant for the requested search. Furthermore, if this website was a site on the costs of parking lots in the Netherlands, it may not have provided trustworthy information.

Defining Search Queries

Defining search queries is a step that revealed large differences between the subjects in our performance tests. Fifty-six percent of the subjects performed search operations using search queries that did not fit the information problem or were overly general. When searching for the restaurant with the most Michelin stars in the city of Amsterdam, it was not uncommon for a respondent to enter very broad keywords such as "restaurant" into the Google search box. When asked to find the country's official minimum wage, the respondents used keywords such as "money" or "salary." These very broad keywords resulted in overly abundant result lists without any relevant information. In some instances, the respondents entered the whole assignment text in the search box. Performance tests conducted among secondary school students (Van Deursen & Van Diepen, 2013) revealed that this method seems to be quite common in this user group. Other studies found that children often use full sentences rather than keywords (e.g., Bilal, 2000).

Most of the subjects only used one or two terms per query. This appears to be typical for Internet users (e.g., Aula & Nordhausen, 2006; Spink, Wolfram, Jansen, & Saracevic, 2001). Of note, Google recognizes over 30 words entered in a query. Using only one or two keywords will often not result in the desired search outcome. As we will demonstrate in chapter 5, search engines increasingly attempt to overcome this skill insufficiency by suggesting preprogrammed keywords. This indeed seems to result in more focused searches (sometimes also from a commercial perspective). A large-scale study among students revealed that 40 percent of the subjects entered multiple search terms, 44 percent identified a statement that captured the demands of the assignment, 48 percent selected a reasonable but overly broad statement, and 8 percent selected statements that did not address the assignment (Katz, 2007).

When the subjects' original searches did not lead to the desired information, some of them only made minor changes to the keywords used. Unfortunately, the small amendments often failed to assist in achieving more appropriate results. Several studies revealed that most people do not attempt alternate search queries when an initial search attempt is unsuccessful (De Vries, Van Der Meij & Lazonder, 2008; Dinet, Favart, & Passerault, 2004).

To conduct a more refined search, people have several options. One option is to use Boolean operators. In our tests, these were barely employed.

Beitzel, Jensen, Chowdhury, Grossman, and Frieder (2004) concluded that only approximately 2 percent of the queries contain such operators. The use of Boolean operators is more common in the searches of people who received training in search system use. However, people who received training require periodic refresher courses on proper Boolean operator usage (Siegfried, Bates, & Wilde, 1993). Boolean operators are neglected by most information searchers. This is unfortunate because even simple operators such as quotation marks could produce substantially more relevant results.

Another option to refine a search is to use advanced searches, such as entering additional criteria such as a date, location, or format. Furthermore, some search engines offer the possibility to search within search results. In the performance tests, the subjects did not employ these advanced options. It appears that most users accept the search system's default values (Markey, 2007). In a study among students, Ivanitskaya, O'Boyle, and Casey (2006) found that only few used advanced search options or limited their searches. Many seemed to rely on basic searches. Overall, it appears that people seldom apply advanced search features when they conduct online searches (e.g., Bishop et al., 2000; Jansen, 2005; Spink et al., 2001).

Selecting Relevant Search Results

Search engines return a vast number of unsuitable search results, especially when people do not define a proper search query. Thus, the intensive selection of proper search results is required. Our tests reveal that Internet users are overly confident in the search engines' ability to provide high-quality results. In two cases, the subjects even used the Google option "I'm feeling lucky" (we wonder why this option is provided at all). Needless to say, this option offers no control over the destination. Most of the subjects examined only the top two or three results. Looking beyond the first page of results was a peculiarity. Sponsored or commercial results, listed at the top of the Google search result pages, were opened by over half of the respondents in one of the search assignments. Jansen and Spink (2003) reported that, on average, search engine users view approximately two to three documents per query, over 55 percent of searchers view only one result per query, and more than 66 percent examine fewer than five documents in a given session.

Evaluating Information Sources

Traditional media literacy notions are concerned with a critical approach to content encountered in the media. Several studies express concerns about the dubious nature of available information on the Internet, complemented by the users' inability to validate or evaluate this information. The results of our performance tests correspond with most studies addressing the evaluation of information retrieved online, namely, that people experience difficulties in such evaluations. In fact, scarcely any assessment of quality, reliability, or accuracy of information found on the web occurs (e.g., Fiegen, Cherry, & Watson, 2002). In our tests, almost none of the subjects seemed to pay attention to the source of the information found. Often, they were happy to find an answer, and it did not matter where the information came from or who wrote it. For example, in the first performance test concerning governmental information, some subjects believed that they found the answer on a website containing classroom talks of primary school pupils. Few people verify retrieved information on another website, even when this information is used for making important decisions (as part of the strategic skills).

Other studies that focus on the evaluation of online information are typically conducted among university student populations. These studies show that even in this context, evaluation is problematic. Students are frequently deceived when viewing online content and are not able to judge the validity of a website (e.g., Leu et al., 2007). Scott and O'Sullivan (2005) concluded that "any information is attributed to be good information, and the more of it, the better" (p. 22). There is little to no evidence that students spontaneously evaluate information found on the basis of other available attributes of the source that may affect the interpretability of the source (Britt & Aglinskas, 2002; Lorenzen, 2002). Even when evaluation occurs, unfortunately, the evaluation may be incorrect. In an assignment in which students were specifically asked to evaluate a set of websites, 52 percent judged the objectivity of the sites correctly, 65 percent judged the authority correctly, 72 percent judged the timeliness correctly, and overall, only 49 percent uniquely identified the one website that met all criteria (Katz, 2007).

Levels of Communication Internet Skills

In this section, we will discuss the different aspects related to communication Internet skills. We have not yet measured these skills in performance tests and overall, little empirical data are available, making communication Internet skills an important area for the research agenda of the future.

Search, Select, Evaluate, and Act upon Contacts Online (Networking)

Managing online contacts is a prominent skill component in the use of social networking sites, which allows users to invite others to their contact list. Creating, maintaining, expanding, and reducing contacts are all necessary communication skills in using such sites. In social network sites, contacts are often labeled as "friends," which is somewhat misleading because the connection does not necessarily indicate friendship in the everyday sense (Boyd, 2006). Research shows that users connect to both people who they already know offline (e.g., friends, acquaintances, family members, or colleagues) and new connections made online (Chen, Geyer, Dugan, Muller, & Guy, 2009).

The reasons people connect are varied. One reason might be a desire to observe an individual's private profile. Another reason might be feelings that it is socially inappropriate to reject someone familiar as a contact (Boyd, 2007). Status is also an important motive to connect to others; having many "friends" makes someone more socially desirable (Ellison, Steinfield, & Lampe, 2007). After all, the number of contacts (including names and other details) is visible to people who are both inside and outside of the network. Not everyone takes the process of making contacts online seriously or has sufficient contact management skills. Some social network sites reinforce these shortcomings by offering tools that allow users to invite friends in bulk, for example, using a user's email account to search for contacts, who are subsequently invited by email to the social network. The result is a long list of online contacts, scarcely categorized as, for example, siblings, lovers, schoolmates, or strangers. In most instances, all contacts are labeled in the same manner and placed in one category, making it difficult to manage. The number of contacts often seems more important than the quality of the contacts. However, despite having such a large number of contacts, most users only have contact with a few people who are close to them (e.g., Golder, Wilkinson, & Huberman, 2007).

On Twitter, even though users declare that they follow many people, they only keep in touch with a small number of them (Huberman, Romero, & Wu, 2009). This also occurs in the use of mobile phones. A casual search through recent calls made through any mobile phone typically reveals that a small percentage of the contacts stored in the phone are frequently contacted by the user (Huberman et al., 2009). The reduction of the number of contacts only occurs after improper behavior or the passing away of a friend (and sometimes not even on that occasion).

The lack of contact management skills among users of social network sites is not surprising. The explicit listing and categorization of contacts is a new phenomenon that scarcely existed in traditional social networking. Because social networking sites are quite large, finding interesting contacts is not easy. We believe that many users have difficulties in being selective because the supply is overwhelming. This is also true in the way people use email. Email lists of contacts are not, or only messily, maintained and CCs and BCCs are used excessively.

The selection and evaluation of contacts online also contains aspects of strategic skills, as they refer to the goals of users in utilizing social network sites. However, reactions to contact invitations and reply messages are clearly communication skills.

Encode, Decode, and Exchange Messages Online, or Construct, Understand, and Exchange Meaning

Communication on the Internet largely occurs through the use of a keyboard. Facial expressions, body language, or tonal inflections are often absent. The purpose of (online) communication is to convey a message clearly and unambiguously. This requires effort from both the sender (the encoder) and the receiver (the decoder). Both must attach the same meaning to the message. If encoding or decoding fails, the message sent does not necessarily match the message received, causing a communication failure. Online communication is often slower, although it can be real-time in online chat or telephony, and nonverbal communication is often absent (making emotional information unavailable); thus, online communication requires additional skills.

The communication encoder is responsible for transferring the information that he/she wants to send to a receiver into a form that can be correctly decoded at the other end. Conveying information clearly is not easy and is especially difficult for people who are not accustomed to online communication. Because the potential audience on the Internet is quite large, people often do not know with whom they are communicating (e.g., in public discussion groups and on Twitter). Often, delivered messages are misunderstood.

Just as encoding is a skill, decoding is a skill at the receiver's end. Decoding involves, for example, taking the time to read an online message carefully, listen actively, or watch closely. Confusion can arise from decoding errors when the decoder does not have sufficient domain expertise or lacks an understanding of the context in which the message is created. The short, cryptic messages used in Twitter, for example, not only make encoding difficult (am I writing what I want to say?) but also make decoding difficult (what exactly is he or she saying here?). The newly developed codes used in online chat and SMS increase the difficulty. For many people, these codes are impossible to decode (although sometimes this is the whole point). Furthermore, posts on discussion forums and instant message communications are difficult to decode correctly because these messages mostly lack nuance and score high on the level of ambiguity.

Although additional signals are developed to add more context to textual posts, such as emoticons, having a clear understanding of both the message and the context is difficult. We believe that it is safe to say that some individuals do not have sufficient skills to understand the argument of the person who encoded the message, identify the exact purpose behind a message, or critically evaluate a received message. Furthermore, Internet conversation often lacks politeness because it is direct and abrupt. Messages can easily be misunderstood or taken more literally or rationally than intended. Emotion and humor are easily overlooked. We believe that understanding messages in online environments is especially difficult for people who did not grow up using them.

Attract Attention Online

Of all things being said on the Internet, what is heard? How many of the videos created are being watched? Who is reading your weblog? While traditional views assume that only a few people in society have the skills to spread ideas to others, attracting attention seems to be an even scarcer resource in the digital era. With the massive amount of expressions, opinions, and creations online, standing out is difficult. The vast majority of expressions on the web simply have no or very few receivers. Many postings to online forums have no readership. The bulk of Twitter messages simply melt into thin air. The authors cannot control this; it is a structural limitation of the Internet that expressions are easily made on this medium and average reception is limited by default. Of course, not everyone is looking for fame. Some texts are written by users with only a small audience in mind, for example, travel blogs intended to update friends and family about one's whereabouts. However, it remains difficult to write an attractive text, also for a small intended audience.

In his book *The Myth of Digital Democracy*, Hindman (2009) argues that the political promise of the Internet has gone unfulfilled. "Most online content receives no links, attracts no eyeballs and has minimal political relevance" (p. 18). The Internet is subject to power-law distributions; thus, a small percentage of sites receive the vast percentage of visitors (Hindman, 2009). This leads to "starkly inegalitarian outcomes" (Hindman, 2009, p. 41). Other studies, outside the political context, confirm that weblog popularity follows a power-law distribution, with most of the readership focusing on a small group of highly successful weblogs (e.g., Shirky, 2003;

Sifry, 2005). In fact, power laws are applicable to several online aspects, including videos posted on sites such as YouTube. Many videos have only been watched by the uploader. Related to this phenomenon is the use of tagging, in which keywords are assigned to, for example, bookmarks, images, or video files. Tagging aids in describing such items and allows it to be found again when browsing or searching. The ability to create effective tags is not simple but is required to attract people to uploaded files. Studies reveal that both the amount of tagging and the quality of tags used are inadequate (e.g., Sigurbjörnsson & Van Zwol, 2008).

Construct Online Profiles and Identities

Social networking sites, online dating sites, and virtual worlds offer users several aids in creating an online profile. Most sites provide a template in which users are asked for various types of personal information such as relational status, education, religion, political affiliation, or favorite movies and music. Users are free to provide such information and to post pictures of their choice. It seems quite simple. After all, users have more control over their self-presentational behavior than they would have in face-to-face communication (Ellison, Heino, & Gibbs, 2006). They have the opportunity to determine which aspects of their personalities should be presented and which photos convey the best images; thus, they can manage their self-presentations more strategically than in face-to-face situations (Ellison et al., 2006).

However, do people strategically manage their self-presentations? The information posted on profiles differs immensely. It can be limited to minor details such as gender; it can be tame, such as providing pictures of a pet cat; or it can be extreme, such as providing comments or pictures of alcohol abuse and sexual activities. Peluchette and Karl (2007) found that 42 percent of students using Facebook had comments regarding alcohol, 53 percent had photos involving alcohol use, 20 percent made comments regarding sexual activities, 25 percent had seminude or sexually provocative photos, and 50 percent included some type of curse. A simple glance at some of the profiles on social network sites immediately reveals how amateurish and even clumsy people can be in creating personal images. Online profiles are characterized by grammar mistakes and inappropriate pictures or curses. Some individuals do not understand the permanent nature of Internet posts or consider how they will be viewed by colleagues or potential employers. The result is a gross gray average of profiles and a few conspicuous profiles that attract attention. It is easier to leave online profile information untouched than to update it. Many people simply lack the communication skills for impression management. Why do people post images, text, or videos that may be potentially embarrassing? We speculate that the reason for this is that in our individualized society, people reason from their own perspective and not from the audience's perspective. However, we realize that many people, especially teens and adolescents, use the Internet to discover and build their own identity. Postings on the Internet increasingly have an expressive function.

The amount of online profiles that reveal inappropriate content indicates that users do not seem to be aware of the potential impact that online information might have. A lack of knowledge, rather than a lack of concern, accounts for the risky online behaviors of young adults (Hoofnagle, King, Li, & Turrow, 2010). This is also true for privacy settings, which are used to provide access to online profiles. Even young people who were technically skilled had a hard time in understanding and using the privacy settings on social networking sites (Livingstone, 2008). Many young people consider the Internet as their own personal space where they interact with their peers and fail to recognize that the information intended for peer groups, as well as conversations among peers, are available to many other, unintended audiences (Ito et al., 2008).

Self-presentation in online profiles is quite explicit in the dating arena. Skillful self-presentation is vital in the beginning stages of relationships because daters will use any information available to determine whether to pursue the relationship (Derlega, Winstead, Wong, & Greenspan, 1987). Overall, identity management is an important skill that seems to be underdeveloped in the general Internet user. People should have a profound understanding of how posted online information may be misinterpreted by both an unknown and known audience.

Advanced Communication Skills

In the prior chapter, we defined four advanced communication skills, as proposed by Jenkins et al. (2009). These skills touch upon strategic Internet skills and cannot be expected to be commanded by average users. They are relevant for a small portion of the general Internet user population. These skills cause difficulties for average users, although, to our knowledge, these difficulties have not been explicitly measured from a skill point of view. The first advanced communication skill described was the ability to adopt alternative online identities for discovery or improvisation. We believe that these skills are much better developed in younger users, as they are part of their personal growth path. Even younger users must learn these skills and correct the many pitfalls in the making of their identity online, especially when they are confronted by people with bad intentions. The second skill was the capacity of online communication in the context of simulation, gaming, and experimentation to enable better decision-making. Simulations and games are a good learning experience (Jenkins et al., 2009). However, many users take the underlying models and assumptions as facts. They should be able to analyze and weigh what is real about them. This requires critically assessing their reliability and credibility (Jenkins et al., 2009). We expect that this requires a high level of information and strategic skills (strategic skills are only mastered by a minority of mainly highly educated Internet users).

There are also the communication skills to pool knowledge and exchange meaning with others in peer-to-peer networking, also known as collective intelligence. Examples of collective intelligence are Wikipedia, Flickr, YouTube, Del.icio.us and last.fm, services in which users add valuable information by making social annotations. The skills needed to participate in collective intelligence are summarized by Pierre Lévy in an interview by Rheingold (2012): "The essence of this new skill is to create a synergy between personal knowledge management and collective knowledge management. You have to connect to people and find information sources, then filter, select and categorize information for your own purposes. You have to decide which information to accumulate personally, to store or memorize. When you do this, you can share your personal knowledge with knowledge communities through social bookmarking or blogging or Twitter" (p. 160).

Reasoning from the evidence on information skills discussed in the prior section, we might question whether participating in collective intelligence is achievable by the average Internet user. Collective intelligence requires users to parse problems into distinct parts. It also requires users to interact with others in an appropriate fashion when spreading the identified problems to others with specific expertise. Finally, the collective results must be evaluated. All of these steps present difficulties. The goal is to produce more intelligence than would have been accomplished as an individual. There are several indications that for many, collective intelligence is overly difficult. Forum discussions, for example, tend to be one way, incomplete and interrupted or have broken threads (Hou & Wu, 2011). Furthermore, there is an ongoing debate about the quality of the knowledge on wikis, discussion forums, and other online collaboration platforms, which are typically not subject to editorial control (Bean & Hott, 2005; Long, 2006). Moreover, it appears that people are reluctant to change other people's contributions when using a Wiki (e.g., Danis & Singer, 2008). Furthermore, we wonder whether the use of discussions forums online encourage people to actually "listen" to each other. Often this use seems more focused on stating an individual opinion.

An important reason why collective intelligence seems to only be suited for small portions of the Internet population is that most contemporary education focuses on training autonomous problem solvers and is not well suited to equip students with the skills necessary for collective intelligence (Jenkins, 2006). "We are just learning how to exercise that power—individually and collectively—and fighting to define the terms under which we will be allowed to participate." (p. 245). It seems increasingly likely that the formal education system will need to include both instruction and practice in how to construct and contribute to collective intelligence (McGonigal, 2008).

The final advanced communication skill mentioned in the prior chapter was the ability to exchange meaning to reach decisions and realize transactions while understanding the meanings of others/partners. This strongly relates to levels of strategic skills.

Levels of Content Creation Internet Skills

In chapter 2, we claimed that creating content of high quality requires substantial skills despite the variety of online tools offered to facilitate the process. Of note, here, we focus on the quality of the created content, not on attracting attention after publishing the content. The latter is part of communication skills, as described in the prior section. As the quality of a creation increases, the impact of the intended message increases. Furthermore, because content creation is quickly gaining popularity, Internet users' expectations about the quality is constantly increasing. Creating content of high quality requires more digital tools and a greater understanding and context to use the latest applications than does consumption (Schradie, 2011). To our knowledge, differences in the quality of created content have not been investigated from a digital skills point of view. Thus far, most attention has been concentrated on the identity of content creators.

EU data (Eurostat statistics) reveal that in 2012, 32 percent of all individual Internet users reported having uploaded self-created content. Males reported slightly more self-created content than females. Age reveals large differences, with almost no one creating content above the age of 55. The higher the level of education, the more individuals create content online. US data reveal similar patterns. In 2012, 30 percent of all Internet users indicate to have shared self-created content online (Pew Internet and American Life Project, 2012).

Several theorists of culture have explored what it means to be a producer, but have not investigated the importance of one's socioeconomic status (Schradie, 2011). The figures above reveal that some individuals are not involved in online content creation. Schradie (2011) concluded that as creative content applications and uses increase, the poor and working class have not been able to use these production applications at the same rate as other uses or users. As in other studies, education appears to be an important contributor (e.g., Hargittai & Walejko, 2008). Active content creators are a minority of Internet users and tend to have higher socio-demographic status than the broader Internet-using populations they come from (Brake, 2014). Schradie further concludes that when people are able to access a computer at multiple places, or with multiple gadgets, frequently throughout the day, they have more control over the production process and can produce more content. Access at a location over which economically disadvantaged people have no control, such as a library or school, limits their likelihood of producing online content. Therefore, Schradie indicates that getting online does not automatically lead to content production. We would like to add that creating content does not automatically mean creating content of acceptable quality.

It seems that content creation is most popular among young people. This suggests that in educational contexts, in addition to content use and evaluation, greater access to the tools of content creation should be provided. However, as mentioned, these figures and differences mainly provide information about the identity of the content creators. The figures do not provide information regarding the level of advancement of content creation skills or the quality of the created content. Videos uploaded on YouTube are often characterized by low quality because they are limited by online bandwidths, and the average Internet user has no experience or training in how to direct, edit, and store videos. Video sharing (and other social networking sites) mainly focuses on amateur content. This is also true for online photos and images. Many are satisfied if a video or photo contains the intended object. Most people do not have a creative background and fail to see that the overall creation is simply unattractive. This can also be applied to text writers. The Internet is characterized by poorly constructed texts and spelling mistakes that frustrate readers. Most people are not professional writers. In taking simple photos and subsequently sharing them on social media, most individuals will succeed. Going beyond this amateur production, however, seems to be a step that is mainly reserved for professionals.

Creative usage requires skills that people with more education are expected to possess, such as complex writing, grammar, and comprehension (Schradie, 2011). Most of the content creators will not feel entirely confident with the rapidly changing content production technologies. They will not be able to continually adapt their media production skills. However, as content creation becomes increasingly popular, the quality of the created content must gain greater attention. The current attitude of amateur content creators on the web is satisfaction when they have gone public and reached their practical goals. However, this might change when they are confronted with bad reactions to their products or no reaction at all. Unfortunately, from a digital skills point of view, there is only limited attention to content creation skills, even though numerous handbooks on how to create content exist.

Levels of Strategic Internet Skills

Strategic skills are the most advanced skill set defined in this book. These skills follow information skills, for example, when the searched information is combined, compared, and used to reach an optimal decision. They also follow communication skills, for example, when individuals who meet online are consulted to reach an optimal decision. Finally, they also succeed content creation skills, for example, when online creations are used to reach one's goals in publicity, advertising, or business profit. To adequately perform strategic skills, one requires high levels of all previously mentioned skills. Strategic skills determine the total effect of Internet use. People with a high degree of strategic skills should be able to benefit most from their use of the Internet.

Unfortunately, to our knowledge, there is no research that explicitly addresses these skills on an individual level. We attempted to measure these skills in our performance tests by providing assignments in which users had to make decisions after collecting, combining, and comparing different pieces of information. Assignments, for example, charged subjects with choosing a political party based on three of its social and economic statements, creating a vacation package that was as cheap and attractive as possible, and locating a hospital with the best and fastest treatment of a specific disease. To accomplish such tasks, a high degree of information and communication skills is required. One must be able to combine several pieces of information and draw correct conclusions, create a message that is correctly encoded and decoded to reach a helpful answer at a particular site, and critically evaluate the collected pieces of information. Strategic skills are used to reach the optimal decision.

Strategic skills relate to the usage gap, as defined by Van Dijk (2005) and discussed in chapter 3. It appears that some users utilize the Internet mainly for entertainment purposes, whereas others use capital-enhancing activities that require a higher level of strategic skills. Price comparison on sites and the choice of electronic program guides, for example, also require strategic skills. As we saw in the prior chapter, some users benefit more than others from the Internet overall, that is, in nearly every application. People who fail to benefit from the Internet might lack strategic skills. Our performance tests reveal that these skills are only mastered by a small portion of the general Internet user population. In all performance tests we conducted, an average of 29 percent of the strategic skill assignments were completed correctly. The problems people experienced were quite shocking, as will be explained in the following steps.

The first strategic step required to reach an optimal decision is goal orientation. This refers to awareness of the opportunities offered by the Internet and subsequently determining the goal of the Internet session. In our performance tests, these tasks appeared to be a large problem. Most people do not tend to think much about the desired outcome or fail to set a clear goal; in most cases, they begin the session without specifically thinking about the desired outcome or how it should be achieved. During the task completion, maintaining a required orientation toward the assignment's final goal was difficult. People are easily distracted by irrelevant stimuli on the Internet (e.g., banners with offers or pieces of information containing other interesting topics). Some subjects did not know how to begin the strategic skill assignments, which is not surprising given the problems that people encounter when using their information skills.

The second step in the strategic skill definition is made by taking the correct actions to reach the desired goal. Over one-third of the subjects arrived at websites that support users in making informed decisions (e.g., choosing a political party, an insurance, or healthcare institution). Although these websites might be helpful in making the decisions, people easily take their outcomes for granted. They uncritically used these sites in the basic way that was offered and easily overlooked the frequently present commercial intentions of such sites. Over 90 percent of the subjects who used such websites were not able to generate useful outcomes. To reach an optimal decision, several pieces of information must be compared and combined.

In our tests, we found that 25 percent of the subjects did not combine multiple information sources and used information from only one website. This method was not sufficient to resolve the strategic assignment and gain the intended benefits. Choosing a political party based on three standpoints, for example, requires users to visit the parties' websites and compare their standpoints. Some subjects were convinced that Wikipedia would solve this problem for them. Others began the assignment with typing the URL www.politiek.nl (www.politics.nl), a website that forwarded visitors to a Twitter account with the intention to post sarcastic information about politicians. In general, users tend to become loyal to a single website for accomplishing tasks, even when a better website is available (Zauberman, 2003). Especially for strategic questions, it is important to compare information from different sources to ensure that the potential benefits are optimal (e.g., in comparing holiday trips offered on different websites). In our tests, we found that as age increased, people were less likely to limit their activity to only one website. Finally, we found that over 70 percent of the subjects experienced the problem of working in an unstructured way. Often they tended to surf rather randomly rather than systematically gathering and comparing information piece by piece.

The third step of the decision-making process involves making the right decision to reach the desired goal. This occurs when the required pieces of information are gathered. These pieces of information must be combined and compared so that a decision can be made. Remarkably, we found that even when people collected the right pieces of information, they still experienced problems combining and comparing these pieces to make the best decision. Over 40 percent of the subjects appeared to be making misguided decisions based on the information found. This suggests that even with full information, many people lack the skills to interpret and process the collected pieces correctly, even when the collected information is rather simple. Furthermore, 63 percent of the subjects based their decisions on incomplete information. Of note, some of these decisions were correct, but this was the result of a lucky choice, which subjects did not notice.

Overall, 29 percent of the subjects made the correct decision and consequently would have benefitted from Internet use by achieving the goal. The level of educational attainment appeared to be a decisive factor in the level of strategic Internet skills. Higher educated subjects had a better idea of how to begin the assignment, collect and combine information from multiple sources to reach an optimal decision, and work in a more structured manner. Consequently, they were able to make more correct decisions.

The strategic skill assignments in the performance tests followed logically upon the information skill assignments. We argue that to benefit from online communication or content creation, additional strategic skills are required that are not measured in performance tests yet. In future studies, we will make strategic skills assignments that specifically follow communication and content creation skills. For example, concerning communication skills, we might give subjects assignments to reach as many positive replies as possible to invitations in social networking sites. In measuring content creation skills, we might focus on a given purpose or goal of the created content, such as writing a Twitter message that receives attention.

Internet Skill Inequalities, among Who?

Before conducting the performance tests, we asked respondents for several key demographic and socioeconomic indicators that might affect their levels of Internet skills. The relationship between several indicators and Internet skills were investigated with causal analyses (see Van Deursen et al., 2011). The investigation indicated that age and educational attainment level are the two key indicators that explain differences in Internet skills. Furthermore, the conditional nature of the skills framework was confirmed; the level of the medium-related skills had a large significant effect on the level of content-related Internet skills. This is an important finding, as this strong dependence has major implications concerning the effect of age on Internet skills, as will be explained below.

The first variable under consideration was gender. Women have been slower to begin using the Internet than men; therefore, it is expected that men possess more knowledge about the Internet, resulting in more skillful use (Goulding & Spacey, 2003). Wasserman and Richmond-Abbott (2005) found that the level of Internet use was related to web-knowledge, which was higher among men than among women. Recent studies, however, show little variation by gender in access to the Internet in the developed countries (Eurostat Statistics, 2013; Ono & Zavodny, 2003). One might argue that in most Western countries, educational differences between men and women have largely disappeared. Consequently, Hargittai and Shafer (2006) found that men and women do not differ much in their online abilities; however, women's self-assessed skill levels are significantly lower than those of men. This is consistent with our findings. We did not find gender-related differences in the performances of operational, formal, information, and strategic Internet skills. However, when asked to rate their skill levels prior to the tests in a self-assessment, men rated themselves significantly higher than did women.

Our performance tests did not include the measurement of communication and content creation Internet skills. Thus, the identification of segments that are most in need of these skill improvements is difficult. It is not known how communication and content creation skills are related to more pragmatic informational uses of the Internet. Van Deursen, Courtois, and Van Dijk (2014) suggest that some people turn to communication skills to compensate for shortcomings in information skills. For example, rather than learning how to compose elaborate search queries, one could ask another individual how to find something or how to assess the information available on a website. This could occur by either consulting a support source or employing specific communication Internet skills (e.g., mobilizing a social contact to use effective messages for support questions). The opposite situation may also occur. If one fails to obtain responses from people online, one might compensate by employing information skills to locate a source of helpful information. Furthermore, we should not jump to conclusions based solely on differences in the use of communication or content-related services and applications, as use does not necessarily indicate skillful use. For example, several figures reveal that women favor communication via email and chatting online, sending email, and other computer-mediated communication more than men (e.g., Eurostat Statistics, 2013). However, this does not suggest that women also excel in communications skills as they have defined here. There is little empirical evidence to conclude that men and women differ in the skills of decoding or encoding digital messages or creating an online profile. The same is true for the skills of creating attractive and proper creation. Although men have consistently taken the lead over women concerning offline and online content creation, there seems to be no evidence that the created content is of higher quality than that created by women.

A very strong indicator of operational, formal, information, and strategic Internet skills was the level of educational attainment. The total effect of education on the content-related information and strategic skills resulted from a direct effect of education on these content-related skills complemented with an indirect effect of education via the medium-related operational and formal skills, which were also strongly influenced by educational levels. This is consistent with the assumption that education is a consistent global predictor of the use of ICTs. Individuals with higher levels of education are more likely to have computers and Internet access at home. They also connect more through broadband and spend more time online (e.g., Buente & Robbin, 2008; DiMaggio, Hargittai, Celeste, & Shafer, 2004). Goldin and Katz (2008) argue that more highly educated individuals are able to keep up with technological advancements and, therefore, increase their lead over people who are not able to keep up. Some recent studies that focus on Internet skills confirm this finding (e.g., Gui & Argentin, 2011; Hargittai & Hinnant, 2008), as do the performance test results presented in this chapter. We also believe that education will serve as an important contributor to the levels of communication and content creation skills. The level of education has a positive effect on managing communication in general, including decoding and encoding messages and the other defined communication skills. Furthermore, writing proper and attractive texts is highly related to educational levels of attainment. This might also be the case for creating an attractive online profile, blog, or personal website.

The findings concerning age are particularly remarkable. Young Internet users are consistently identified as very skillful users of the Internet through terms such as "the digital generation" (Papert, 1996), "the net generation" (Tapscott, 1998), "digital natives" (Prensky, 2001), "thumb tribes" (Rheingold, 2012), "millennials" (Howe & Strauss, 2000), "cyber kids" (Holloway & Valentine, 2003), or "Generation Y" (Jorgenson, 2003). All of these expressions point toward young Internet users' vast amount of exposure to digital and networked media. Because of this exposure, it is often automatically assumed that they are skillful users. Older people, on the contrary, are considered to be laggards in the diffusion process of new innovations. They did not have the opportunity to acquaint themselves with the Internet at school and lag behind in their ownership and use of computers and the Internet. Furthermore, aging results in more problems with learning digital skills due to decreased working memory and reaction times (Boyd & Bee, 2009). Some recent studies, however, did not reveal a relationship between Internet skills and one's age (e.g., Bullen, Morgan, & Qayyum, 2011; Hargittai, 2010; Helsper & Eynon, 2010; Jones, Ramanau, Cross, & Healing, 2010). The findings of our performance tests go even further and indicate that some serious reconsiderations are necessary. As shown in this chapter, operational and formal Internet skill deficiencies primarily occur among seniors and less educated portions of the population. Path analysis revealed a strong and significant direct negative effect of age on these medium-related skills (see Van Deursen et al., 2011). Therefore, with increases in age, it becomes increasingly important to improve medium-related skills because these are basic requirements to perform the higher order information, communication, content creation, and strategic Internet skills.

However, the results of our performance tests also revealed that there is much room for improvement concerning the content-related information and strategic Internet skills of young people. First, it is important to acknowledge that young people experience content-related skills problems, despite their technical prowess. In fact, conducted path analysis revealed a strong significant *positive* effect of increasing age on the content-related information and strategic skills (see Van Deursen et al., 2011). This result indicates that older people perform better with regard to these skills! There is, however, an important caveat resulting from the conditional nature of the Internet skills definition. Although older people display better content-related Internet skills, their efforts are thwarted by their impaired medium-related skills. Aging results in such an amount of medium-related skill problems that the positive effect on the content-related skills is neutralized.

These results indicate that younger people must be taught better information and strategic Internet skills. Conversely, elderly people must learn medium-related skills more effectively because impairment in these skills hinders their performance on the content-related Internet skills.

Recommendations on how to account for these shortcomings are provided in chapters 5 and 6.

These surprising results strengthen the importance of measuring Internet skills comprehensively and in detail, considering the full range of Internet skills proposed in this book. This need becomes even more apparent when considering self-ratings of Internet skills. We found that subjects in the youngest age group(s) rate themselves significantly higher than subjects in the oldest age group(s). Thus, subjects primarily considered operational skills when assessing their level of Internet skills. These are the areas in which subjects in the youngest group performed best. Often, self-assessments of Internet skills seem to focus on this so-called button knowledge, providing an incorrect view of the level of Internet skills. The danger is that content-related skills might be easily overseen and neglected in policy decisions.

Regarding the relation between age and communication skills, one might argue that people who have grown up in a digital environment and those who are constantly communicating over the Internet might develop these skills more rapidly. There is substantial evidence that younger people more often use online communication technologies, such as instant messaging and chat, than do older people (e.g., Lenhart, Madden, & Hitlin, 2005; Valkenburg & Peter, 2007). However, especially for the more advanced communication skills, the same effect as described above concerning the information and strategic skills might appear. Aging might result in a more critical look at ways of communication and what is being said to whom. It might also result in much better and more carefully designed online profiles or better negotiation tactics. Experience in life certainly has some advantages here.

Content creation requires the use of various production tools that require additional operational skills. These skills decrease with aging. In particular, video or image editing or remixing multimedia might be activities that younger people learn quickly. However, the skills to write proper texts, take photos of high quality, and create attractive videos might increase with age, although aging seems to result in less participation in online content creation.

Internet experience and time spent online are also often mentioned as factors that influence the levels of Internet skills. People who spend more time online—whether at work or another location—will acquire more knowledge about the Internet and thus develop better online skills (Hargittai, 2002). Moreover, people who have been Internet users for a longer period of time are expected to be better at locating information online because they have more experience to draw upon (Hargittai, 2002). In general, for both computers and the Internet, the length of previous experience and the amount of current usage have been associated with greater technological expertise.

However, the overall findings of our performance tests revealed that Internet experience contributed only to the medium-related skills. We did not find an effect of time spent online in two out of three studies. The analyses made it clear that the content-related information and strategic Internet skills do not seem to improve with years of Internet experience or the amount of time spent online weekly. This finding again stresses the importance of distinguishing between several types of Internet skills.

The effect of level of educational attainment often intertwines with other constructs such as income, occupation, and ethnicity. Research reveals differences in types of usage across these variables; however, to our knowledge, it has not yet been specifically investigated whether this is a direct result of skill differences. The difference might also relate to motivation and interest. The effects of occupational position and income in our studies seem to be a result of level of education. We did not find an independent effect of position or income on any of the measured Internet skills.

The existence of a racial divide has been documented more intensively in the United States than in Europe. Several studies indicate racial differences in rates of computer and Internet use. In almost all data on use, minorities such as blacks, Hispanics, or Asians are often underrepresented. However, there seems to be an exception for communication and content creation activities. The Pew Internet and American Life Project's survey, for example, found that these minorities are more involved in content creation and social media use than native users (Correa, Willard Hinsley, & Gil de Zuniga, 2010; Lenhart, 2009). Concerning the measurements of skills, however, reliable data are lacking. In an investigation among students, Hargittai (2010) revealed that students of lower socioeconomic status, Hispanic origin, and African Americans exhibit lower levels of Web know-how than others.

Hopefully, one day, the degree of Internet skill levels by diverse demographic groups will be as well documented as home access to computers and the Internet.

Conclusions

In this chapter, we presented empirical evidence on the levels of command that the general Internet user population currently shows concerning the six types of Internet skills. Much of the evidence presented is the result of performance tests conducted among a large sample of the Dutch population, complemented with other empirical studies that provide information on the levels of the six Internet skills. The general conclusion of this chapter is that the original digital divide (defined as the gap between people who have and do not have physical access to computers and the Internet; see also figure 1.1) has now developed a divide that includes differences in the skills needed to use the Internet. A second important conclusion follows from the empirical confirmation to consider both medium- and content-related Internet skills. In contemporary (and future) information society, it is the content-related skills that increasingly determine people's positions in the labor market and in social life. Unfortunately, these skills appear to be the most problematic, and many seem to be struggling to equip themselves with the skills they need to participate in contemporary society. The presented evidence strongly indicates that large portions of the population will be excluded from actual and effective Internet use. Continuing the transformations toward the Internet in the most important domains of life will eventually lead to serious problems if the lack of Internet skills among large portions of the population is not accounted for. Unfortunately, only the lack of operational and formal Internet skills might be considered as a temporary problem (until a more accessible technology appears). The lack of information, communication, content creation, and strategic skills seems to be more structural. These skills are strongly related to education and intellectual capacities. While the digital divide could originally be "easily" addressed by providing physical access, this problem now seems to be much more difficult when content-related Internet skills are considered.

The evidence for the Internet skill levels as presented in this chapter reveals that, contrary to what research using self-reports concludes, there are small differences in the Internet skills between men and women. Age appears to have a negative influence on medium-related operational and formal Internet skills. Seniors especially struggle regarding these skills. Although newer technologies present features such as touchscreens that provide some support for the problems seniors encounter, the decreasing sizes of the displays again make things more difficult for them. However, concerning age, the most important finding is that there is a positive contribution to the level of content-related information and strategic skills, meaning that older generations perform better on these skills than younger generations. Unfortunately, the older generations are impeded by their low level of medium-related skills in such a way that the actual result is negative. This conclusion has hardly received any attention. If people in older groups improve their medium-related Internet skills, they are likely to perform better on the information and strategic Internet skills than the younger generations. For all Internet skills, less-educated populations seem to struggle most. While these groups have always been socially disadvantaged, their life chances are now in greater danger. These groups are increasingly excluded from all of the benefits the Internet now has to offer (see chapter 3). Because the amount of Internet use or experience also seems to have only minor effects (especially on content-related Internet skills), the evidence provided contrasts somewhat with the idea that people learn digital skills more through practice than in formal educational settings. Content-related Internet skills do not seem to increase with years of Internet experience or the number of hours spent online per week.

Further Reading

- Van Deursen, A. (2010). *Internet skills, vital assets in an information society.* Enschede: University of Twente.
  PhD dissertation that lies at the base of this book. Detailed results of the performance tests are provided.
- Goldin, C., & Katz, L. F. (2008). *The race between education and technology.* Cambridge, MA: The Belknap Press of Harvard University.
  An historical analysis of the coevolution of educational attainment and wage structures.
- Schradie, J. (2011). The digital production gap: The digital divide and Web 2.0 collide. *Poetics, 34*(4–5), 221–235.
  Digital inequality research with a focus on production to examine who is creating digital content for the public sphere. The results point to a class-based gap among producers of online content.
- Litt, E. (2012). Measuring users' Internet skills: A review of past assessments and a look towards the future. *New media and society, 15*(4), 612–630.
  A literature overview on measurements of everyday users' basic Internet skills.
- Walraven, A., Brand-Gruwel, S., & Boshuizen, H. P. A. (2008). Information-problem solving: A review of problems students encounter and instructional solutions. *Computers in Human Behavior, 24*(3), 623–648.
  Another review, this time to determine what kinds of problems are encountered when using the Internet for searching information.

CHAPTER 5

Solutions: Better Design

Introduction

In the chapter 3, we established that the consequences of insufficient levels of digital skills are exclusion from the contemporary and future information-based society. These skills are the key to the information society. Therefore, there is a strong need for policies that attempt to compensate for low levels of these skills, especially policies aimed at those with the greatest need. Because the levels of Internet and other digital skills differ among segments of the population, it is necessary to utilize a variety of treatments. Thus, digital skills are a complex policy problem that calls for both technological and educational solutions. Livingstone (2003) considers literacy to be an emergent property of the interaction and mutual dependence between people and ICT. Therefore, communication failures may be as much a result of poor interface design as of poor education. However, in discussions of the population's failure to achieve certain levels of literacy, it is implicitly assumed that interfaces are well designed and merely await appropriate use (Livingstone, 2003). Although it is unknown how poorly designed interfaces and contents of low quality interact with levels of digital skills, it might be expected that people with low levels of skills experience additional difficulty.

In this chapter, we discuss possible improvements in interface development. This is done from a medium-related skills perspective. Experienced operational and formal skill-related problems point toward recommendations that developers might consider when designing new services and applications. This chapter continues with a discussion on improving online content. The provided content should be understandable and suitable for the public for which it is intended. The improvement of online content is discussed from an information, communication, content creation and strategic skills perspective.

Improving Interface Development

It is important for designers to understand that a significant number of people, especially those with lower levels of educational attainment and the elderly, possess insufficient levels of operational and formal Internet skills to guarantee a successful Internet session. In chapter 4, we concluded that older Internet users outperformed younger users with regard to information and strategic Internet skills, as the elderly were not hindered by their limited possession of operational and formal skills. Therefore, seniors will especially benefit from web applications and services that account for lower levels of operational and formal Internet skills. The web is no longer exclusively used by young and middle-aged people, as adults over the age of 65 have discovered the Internet and their usage figures rise every year. Altogether, there is a strong call for designers to cater websites to the specific needs of older visitors. Designers often seem to lack the understanding that the needs of older people differ from those of their younger counterparts, an important reason for older people's tendency to shy away from the web (Kolodinsky, Cranwell, & Rowe, 2002).

Designers should pay specific attention to users who possess lower levels of operational and formal Internet skills. Often, designers' main focus is creating an attractive design rather than an accessible or user-friendly design. The result is that many people struggle to navigate the Internet because the implemented designs are overly difficult to use. This is worrisome because information and services are often offered online with the expectation that all individuals are able to use them. Over the last few years, similar trends have been observed for applications that are specifically designed for mobile computers.

There are a great number of scientific books and articles on improving interfaces for both desktop and mobile applications. Often, they provide detailed instructions that designers can follow. The guidelines that are offered by the World Wide Web Consortium (W3C) are likely the most well-known. W3C offers a broad range of guidelines in making technology available to and usable by all people regardless of their age, education, abilities, economic situation, geographic location, or language, to name a few. The Web Access Initiative (WAI) is a special working group under the W3C that develops guidelines that are widely considered as the international standard for web accessibility. Although the WAI guidelines primarily concern people with disabilities, they could support a wider range of people, including those who suffer from medium-related skill insufficiencies. The WAI's Web Content Accessibility Guidelines (WCAG) comprise well-developed and detailed checkpoints that designers can use to assure a website's accessibility. There are, for example, details on how to support users in navigation, locating content, or determining their location. Detailed suggestions, for example, include limiting the number of links per page, providing mechanisms to navigate to different sections of the content of a webpage, and making links visually distinct. These recommendations could benefit several subjects who participated in the current study's performance tests, certainly not only people with disabilities. Unfortunately, it seems that most initiatives and guidelines are not taken into sufficient account. Although most countries require websites and other technologies sponsored by the federal government to comply with accessibility guidelines, there seems to be much room for improvement even among these sites, which are intended to deliver services to all individuals.

The large availability of handbooks and guidelines provide a good case that there is room for improvement in today's user interfaces. The results of the performance tests discussed in chapter 4 confirm this notion. During these tests, we discovered that many websites are organized and structured in ways that make them overly inaccessible and difficult to use. People with lower levels of formal Internet skills experienced severe problems when navigating in and between websites and menus, as these sites and menus are not catered to their specific needs. In fact, the number of websites that follow any of the available guidelines is disturbingly low; consequently, there are innumerable inaccessible websites offered online. In interface development processes, designers often claim that they will address accessibility at a later stage; however, this often does not occur due to clients' pressure to publish the website as soon as possible (Powell, 2000). Furthermore, economic setbacks place additional pressure on designers to reduce their costs, which often occurs at the expense of testing for accessibility.

It is beyond the purpose of this book to collect and present various specific design recommendations. Several collections are easily available online, for example, at the W3C website. Our aim is to propose some broader solutions that follow directly from our observations. The most important solution is to take into account various user groups that lack medium-related skills when designing interfaces. Guidelines and policy initiatives often stress the need to account for seniors, differently abled users, and the illiterate. We believe, however, that the group of people that would greatly benefit from improved interfaces is much larger. For example, people with lower levels of education also require specific attention. In most developed countries, this group constitutes around one-third of the entire population. In undeveloped countries, the proportion of people with low education levels is even greater.

The idea of accounting for specific groups when designing interfaces is not radically new. In fact, for years, initiatives have existed that specifically aim to support developers in their quest to create a design that accounts for all individuals' needs. One example is The Design for All Foundation. This foundation's mission is to focus on "the intervention on environments, products and services with the aim that everyone, including future generations, regardless of age, gender, capabilities or cultural background, can enjoy participating in the construction of our society, with equal opportunities participating in economic, social, cultural, recreational and entertainment activities while also being able to access, use and understand whatever part of the environment with as much independence as possible." To apply these concepts in products, applications, and services, the foundation stresses that developers should take into consideration the following two simple principles: (1) Make the use of products and services easier for everyone; and (2) Ensure that the needs, wishes, and expectations of users are taken into consideration in the design and evaluation processes of products or services.

In addition to the examples mentioned, there are several other consortiums that offer guidelines on how to make interfaces more accessible. A common belief of most consortiums is that designers should take a User Centered Design (UCD) approach. The goal of this approach is to design with a high degree of usability. In UCD, the end user is placed at the center of the development when the products are intended for human use (Gould & Lewis, 1985). The needs, wants, and limitations of end users are accounted for in all stages of the design process. Rubin (1994) describes the three main principles of UCD, as follows: (1) an early focus on (and understanding of) the users and their tasks; (2) empirical measurement of product usage; and (3) iterative design whereby a product is designed, modified, and tested repeatedly. By employing UCD, designers are forced to test their personal beliefs concerning how others will use their creations. This is necessary because most designers do not instinctively understand how people experience their interfaces. Therefore, usability testing is an important stage in the UCD approach.

Usability testing involves the evaluation of a designed interface by including actual users in the test. Including actual users' results in an understanding of how the interface is used and the problems that people experience. Based on the test results, areas of interface improvement can be identified. Based on the results of the performance tests described in chapter 4, it seems that usability testers should recruit users across a broad spectrum of abilities and not overlook seniors and people with lower levels of education and Internet experience. Whereas younger Internet users might prefer flashy and hip designs, users with lower levels of operational and formal skills might experience difficulties in using such designs. If applications or services are intended for a large variety of (or all) Internet users, then several types of users from the target population should be included in the design process. Especially in the usability testing stage, low-skilled users should be asked to perform representative tasks and observed to determine how they might be supported. In addition to including a wide variety of subjects, qualified usability testers who are capable of conducting tests without biasing the users' behaviors or test materials should be involved in testing.

In an ideal world, all applications and services would be thoroughly tested using UCD principles before becoming public. This might be considered an unrealistic Utopian vision, but some organizations (e.g., government and healthcare organizations) have the responsibility of catering to all users in their service delivery. These organizations should not overlook those with lower levels of medium-related skills. Shockingly, there are many examples of large public organizations that seem to refuse to invest in hiring usability testers. By contrast, commercial organizations often invest large amounts of money in the development and accessibility of their electronic services because the organization's existence depends on these features. In online public service delivery, the focus is often offering as many services as possible rather than the quality of the services in terms of usability or user-friendliness. This quantitative approach can be largely traced back to the existence of various benchmarks that consider the amount of services offered as the most important indicator of online service delivery. Both national and international benchmarks were quite popular at the beginning of this millennium. They continue to exist, but have slowly shifted focus toward the quality of the online services in terms of accessibility and usability. In the first performance test that we conducted, subjects were provided several assignments related to government services. We observed that subjects who visited a number 1 ranked municipal website (as determined in the most important benchmark for public websites in the Netherlands) experienced severe usability-related problems, including the use of a nonfunctioning and slow rollover main menu. Subjects with lower levels of formal Internet skills were hindered to such an extent that they gave up on the assignment. The entire number 1 ranked website was of no use to them. As substantiated in this chapter, several guidelines are proposed to support the development of user-friendly website designs. At a minimum, such guidelines must be employed by developers of federal websites. Unfortunately, the main contribution of most benchmarks is the development of advanced and flashy features rather than the promotion of simplicity and improvements from the user's point of view.

In the context of federal service delivery, the performance tests demonstrated that many governmental websites are organized and structured in ways that make them overly inaccessible and difficult to use considering the complexity of the information offered. This also holds for the excessive number of health-related websites. From a citizen's point of view, one might ask whether it is necessary for all government and health organizations to maintain their own image and profile when they develop and implement web applications and services. Interaction between these organizations and users differs for every service that employs its own design and structure. Consistency in the offered web services would greatly benefit both seniors and lower educated Internet users. Currently, these users must learn things anew with every website or application. Therefore, it might be logical to use the same website structure and design, for example, for every government or healthcare organization (which might even result in cost reductions). The most important goal should be to provide the Internet as a means for simple information retrieval and service supply. When public and health agencies employ websites that are equal in design and structure, the more advanced websites that are present on the Internet could be provided as supplementary for those who require more advanced information and services. Thus, organizations should begin to employ two different websites, one advanced version that accounts for the needs of the Internet users with relatively difficult questions and high levels of skills and a simple version that accounts for the needs of the Internet users with relatively easy questions and lower levels of Internet skills. In the latter version, a recognizable, identical, and simple design that omits options that are barely used should be provided. Furthermore, an "exaggerated" explanation of the operation of the website and the steps that one is able to take would benefit many users. Considering design and a didactic approach, the easy version should the same for every agency. An identical website for different organizations not only reduces developing costs, it also caters to the less operational and formal skilled users, who are traditionally exposed to new challenges on every website. Subsequently, websites with identical interfaces can be linked in a network of government or health websites that covers all basic information and transaction needs. Employing two different websites might seem to be a revolutionary idea for many agencies and developers. However, a complete restructuring of service delivery would be quite helpful for both inexperienced and more experienced users. Currently, the fragmented and supply-oriented nature of the service provision of government departments, which do not sufficiently cooperate, strongly reinforces inaccessibility.

At a minimum, many users require clear feedback on the services that they use. Feedback that indicates whether a search engine is searching or that indicates that no results have been found may seem redundant. However, such feedback is not redundant to people who become confused because they do not know what the website is doing or fear that they are doing something wrong. For example, in the current study, because a search engine did not deliver results in the first two seconds, an 18-year-old participant instantly moved to the next website. By contrast, an 81-year-old subject conducted a search operation that did not provide any results. After five minutes of waiting, he asked whether he could go get a cup of coffee because the "computer was still thinking." If the search engine had clearly indicated that no results had been found, this man would have continued the Internet session.

Another recommendation based on the tests is the provision of explicit options on a website; users should be given a clear and accurate overview of the website or service. This also applies to the provided menus that, in many cases, require a better explanation of the content of each link. Detailed instructions on how to use an online service would benefit many users. This might sound exaggerated from a designer perspective, but both people with low levels of educational attainment and seniors would benefit. Still, some users do not know that search queries do not belong in the address bar or that they should be typed with spaces.

Better Interfaces in Mobile Devices, Smartphones, and Tablets?

To conclude this section, we argue that in addition to the development for online services on large screens such as desktops and laptops, specific attention should be paid to transforming services on mobile devices such as smartphones and tablets. There are several specific guidelines available on how to design for mobile devices (e.g., Gong & Tarasewich, 2004). These guidelines are necessary because designing for relatively small devices is restrictive due to the limited computing power and the constantly changing contexts in which they are used (Tarasewich, 2003). Unfortunately, each mobile device developer employs his own interface design and, therefore, employs different menu structures or interaction methods. In chapter 4, it was established that problems related to navigation and orientation might occur relatively more often on devices with small displays, such as smartphones or tablet PCs. Such devices employ different structures, making browsing a different experience. Although users might become increasingly accustomed to using mobile devices, for many, navigation and orientation do not occur naturally. There is, however, an observable trend in which

Internet services and applications especially designed for devices with small screens seem to limit operational and formal skill requirements by providing a much more intuitive experience.

At the time of writing, the rise of tablets is particularly spectacular. Many users are replacing their PC's and even laptops with tablets. Both (very) young and (very) old are attracted by the apparently easy and intuitively interface of tablets. Some people are tempted to think that these devices will solve the problem of a lack of medium-related digital skills. However, recent research shows that the daily use of this new medium is rather limited. In an intensive dairy study among a small sample of US users, Müller, Gove, and Webb (2012) indicated that 91% of reported tablet use was for personal purposes, while only 9% was related to work. The locus of use is primarily at the home where tablets are finding its way in the living room (couch or table), the bed(room), and the kitchen. Most often they are used while watching TV, cooking, and exchanging and playing with other household members, for example, to educate children. Tablets are also used in offices (particularly in meetings to read documents and make notes), on the go (to read, watch videos, and play games), and in shops (to search product and price information). In the home, applications are predominantly used for fun and relaxation. The most important uses are entertainment (games, music, video), (continually) checking email, social networking, shopping, and searching relatively simple information (Müller et al., 2012). Tablets are used for reading, searching information, and making notes, but less for typing long documents or emails and advanced tasks for work. Müller et al. (2012, p. 9) observed that typing on the tablet is a pain point and that users find it frustrating that tablets are limited for data entry.

Though tablets and some other mobile devices help people to speedily learn basic operational and formal skills and are viable tools for education and cooperative work, they also have a number of disadvantages. In terms of content-related digital skills the deceptive ease of use of tablets also holds an important hidden danger. The discussed type of use above might lead to an increase in the so-called usage gap we discussed in chapter 3. We claimed that people with better social positions and higher education use significantly more so-called serious Internet applications that help them in their work, careers, business, and studies, whereas people with lesser positions and lower education use more applications for entertainment, simple communication, and shopping. Mossberger, Tolbert, and Hamilton (2012) observed that online activities in mobile access only were significantly different from home broadband. Mobile use was between 10 to 20 percent lower for the following activities: community, government and political information, online news, and work-related activities. The only more serious and career-related activity on a mobile device was searching for job information and applying for a job. Online entertainment activities in the use of mobile devices (video, music, games, and SNS) were 5 to 12 percent more frequent than in home broadband use (Mossberger et al., 2012). So, the problem of tablets with their relatively easy and intuitive use of these media promotes a more consumptive, instead of productive and creative use. The suggested usage patterns of the programs and apps on these devices are simply followed. The result is that the freedom in performing content-related skills on such devices and having a user-generated creative input is much more controlled and limited by the application itself than in desktops and laptops with complete functionality. Thus, the shift toward mobile devices might even accelerate the usage gaps. This time the gap will be between people who use desktop computers and laptops with advanced functions, on the one hand, and people who rely on mobile devices with limited and largely preprogrammed functions, on the other hand.

Improving Online Content

In this section, we focus on the content provided by the interface, for example, texts, photos, videos, or images. Ciolek (1996) predicted that the sum of uncoordinated activities of a large number of people who use the web would result in a nebulous, ever-changing multitude of websites that store information that is constantly changing. Indeed, individuals' ability to overcome the many challenges of online content largely depends on their level of content-related skills. In this section, we discuss difficulties that surfaced in the information skill performance test findings. Subsequently, we discuss improving content from a communication skills perspective, content creation skills perspective, and strategic skill perspective. Concerning the latter, the performance test results provided several indications of how users might be supported in their quest to gain from the Internet.

Improving Content from an Information Skill Perspective

The performance test showed that the levels of information Internet skills in general appeared to be quite low. Most subjects took a greater number of steps in the search process and used more time than necessary given the difficulty of the assignments. Although a lack of content-related Internet skills was a major cause of these issues, developers' insufficient anticipation of lower levels of these skills seemed to worsen the problem. Improvements in online information provision would benefit many users, especially those with lower and intermediate levels of education. To provide insights on how online information provision might be improved, we focus on the information-seeking process proposed in chapter 2. Each step of this process provides indications on how the functionality of existing search systems and information provision in general can be improved.

The first step from which developers can take clues is the source that users select to collect the desired information. Ideally, after selecting a source, users obtain immediate access to the desired information. It is advisable for designers to include the main topics in the first few lines of text on the home page. Furthermore, search facilities should be placed in a noticeable location, as some users prefer to search than to browse. Users automatically turn to several large-scale portals when searching for a specific piece of information. Although the development of online portals may be a well-intentioned attempt to create order in the chaos, these portals often seem to fail in making things easier for its users. Typically, the scope of information and the menu designs are overly broad. As revealed in the performance test results, many users experience difficulty in locating the relevant pieces of information due to the excessive amount of information collected and offered on these portals. Therefore, as substantiated in the prior section, organizations should carefully consider the added value of a portal before developing such a site. At a minimum, portals should state their purposes, who offers them and what people might expect.

Portals often do not achieve their goal and, in most cases, they are not people's first choice in searching for information. In the performance tests, we allowed users to choose their preferred method of locating information. They did not utilize various portals and special sites; rather, they turned directly to Google. People use their preferred search engines and accommodate their methods of information supply to these engines. For many users, Google is the point of departure; therefore, developers might find it useful to monitor how people first reach their websites. These pages could then be supported as entry points.

The next step in the search process considers the formulation of search queries. Many of the subjects in the performance tests experienced problems in formulating a reasonable search query. This suggests that it is necessary to develop tools that support the query-formulation process. Google, for example, offers such a tool by suggesting queries when words are typed into the search bar. Of note, this tool is not always helpful. At times, users seem to take these suggestions for granted. Furthermore, users who misspell words might be automatically corrected with the correct spelling rather than receiving a "no result" response. There are also several good examples of search engines that provide suggestions when visitors define overly broad queries (Did you mean...?). The mentioned recommendations might be especially helpful for people who have trouble defining clear search queries and selecting relevant search results.

In the step concerning the selection of relevant information or suitable search results, both the quality and amount of online information play an important role. When focusing on the *quality*, it appears that many options that are listed on the search result pages after conducting a search do not provide the information that people actually need. Often, they think they have found an answer they can use, though an outside observer would conclude that a better answer is available when they would have looked a bit further. Many users are satisfied too fast and do not understand that it is difficult to find a good answer in search engines. Furthermore, many people do not seem to be able to differentiate between commercial and noncommercial search results. People rarely venture past the first three search results, which are often marked as commercial but not recognized as such. Search engines should clearly state which search result links are sponsored.

In the prior section, we emphasized the need for User Centered Design (UCD) approaches when developing Internet applications. UCD approaches benefit all users, not only those with lower levels of medium-related operational and formal skills. Furthermore, with this approach, the provided content undergoes a rigorous test. Several institutions focus on improving—mainly textual—contents provided in media outlets. In the United States, for example, the Plain Language Action and Information Network (PLAIN) is a group of federal employees from different agencies who support the use of clear communication in government writing. Another example is the US Department of Health and Human Services, which has developed a research-based how-to guide for creating web content for Americans with limited literacy skills. The resources offered by initiatives such as PLAIN should not be overlooked by communication professionals or web designers, especially those working for official institutions that provide contents that are often overly complex for the target audience. For example, the language used by officials is often not the same language used by the general Internet user. To improve a text's readability, assessments should examine whether texts are easily processed and understood by the intended users. Several measures of text readability are available to aid in estimating a text's difficulty. In the next chapter, we show that large parts of the population—including those in developed countries—face difficulties in activities that involve reading and comprehension, depending on the text length and complexity.

Improving readability should not be limited to legal contexts only. Ideally, all contexts that cater to the general Internet user should improve readability. When considering online content beyond that of official institutions, it is evident that the quality is not of the same standard as, for example, a published book. As discussed in chapter 4, most online content is amateurish. In addition to written content, online photos and videos and communication in web forums are characterized by a high degree of variance in the distribution of quality, from very high to very low, occasionally even abusive. The result is that users addressed face severe hurdles.

Based on the information in chapter 4, we conclude that especially people with lower levels of education experience problems with online content. Educational attainment level is related to levels of literacy. In case of insufficiencies, these levels might cause difficulties with the provided content of various online services and applications. Even more problems arise when focusing on people with a very low level of literacy. In fact, most of the partial and complete illiterate individuals are excluded from online information. In the next chapter we will discuss the digital skills problems of illiterates more in detail, and also provide recommendations on how to account for illiterate individuals from an educational perspective. From a designer's perspective, we stress that future designs of low-literacy interfaces should include a careful selection of icons and visual images that are realistic rather than abstract and closely resemble the intended meaning of the visuals.

When focusing on the *quantity* of online content, the issue of information overload arises, which is the receipt of an overabundance of information into the senses, causing an overwhelming sensation. In this light, again consider the discussion of public government and health services that are characterized by quantitative approaches that aim to offer as many services as possible. As previously stated, this quantitative approach is offered at the expense of a more qualitative approach that focuses on the usability of websites. As a result of the quantitative approach, an excessive amount of information and services are provided to Internet users, who seem to struggle with the multitude of available information. Similar information is available on different websites. This is not problematic for users if the information is complete and reliable. However, it is unclear whether it is necessary to make such a large amount of official information and services available to the general public. In the Netherlands, for example, some municipality websites even provide the option to apply to build a nuclear power plant! We suggest that public initiatives should focus on identifying the specific services that different segments of the population need and/or are interested in. Official organizations should understand that citizens do not perform as many activities on their websites as they do on other websites. In many countries, online official services such as asking questions or giving opinions, sending forms or performing transactions are barely used. Most people only use online public services to find contact information or office hours, or to gather information about products or services (Van Deursen, Van Dijk, & Ebbers, 2006). When focusing on the general Internet user, it would be wise to provide short and focused content.

The final step in the search process involves the evaluation of information. Based on the performance tests and many other studies, it can be concluded that virtually no users evaluate information that is found online. Because many seem to believe that all content on the Internet is true, official websites should apply quality hallmarks that can only be awarded if the content is proven valid and of high quality. Several such marks exist, but the effectiveness of these marks is under discussion. There are agencies that employ their own "quality marks" to convince people to use their services. Therefore, users should be informed about the quality marks that exist. The content of a web service should be carefully tested and continually scrutinized for quality. Healthcare providers, for example, should ensure that patients who use the Internet have access to reliable information to help them understand their disease and possible treatments.

Improving Content from a Communication Skill Perspective

In this section, we provide general suggestions on how to improve online content from a communication skill point of view, and we use the communication Internet skill definition provided in chapter 2.

The definition begins with managing online contacts. In chapter 4, we argued that many people lack the skills to manage contacts. For example, in social networking, users often list all of their contacts under a single label. In this regard, applications that offer the possibility to add to and remove contacts from contact lists might consider further supporting their users by, for example, providing the opportunity to categorize contacts. Supporting and encouraging people to manage their online contacts might help them become more selective in the determining who should receive specific information. The settings of messages for a public and a private audience in SNS could be articulated better, enabling well-considered choices and to prevent public messages that actually are intended for private audiences. Imagine all Facebook contacts gathered together in one large room. All contacts, from partner to parents, from great aunts to nephews, from ex-partners to friends from college, from colleagues at work to friends of friends, would all be seated randomly. Developers should understand that the lack of face-to-face contact makes it difficult for their users to remember that they are speaking to a diverse group of people (from partner to parents, from great aunts to nephews, from ex-partners to friends from college, from colleagues at work to friends of friends), with many potentially negative effects.

The communication skill definition continues with encoding and decoding messages. Online discussions (for example, in forums, news groups, or SNS) are often direct, abrupt, or impolite. People often do not know who they are speaking to and what effects their communication will have. Therefore, in some instances (e.g., public discussion forums), it would be helpful to employ discussion board moderators. The result might be a better understanding of who is active in the discussion and whether an individual's messages must be scrutinized. Such moderators should not limit individuals' freedom of speech, but ensure that the discussion follows general rules of politeness. Moderators can provide users with guidelines or rules, or so-called *netiquette*, the mode of online behavior that should be followed on the forum. Users can subsequently be informed of the existing rules before they begin participating in the discussions. It seems that although several examples of netiquette are provided, most people neglect such recommendations and express whatever they feel is appropriate. Examples of recommendations might be as simple as carefully considering whether the posting of a certain message, photo, or video is suitable given the intended public. Another example is carefully checking whether an intended message indeed reflects the written piece. Finally, grammar checks could be incorporated to automatically suggest corrections for textual user input.

The communication skills definition continues with attracting attention, which is a difficult task for the general Internet user. Numerous Internet marketing agencies attempt to attract customers by promising many visitors to websites or weblogs. Websites that depend on users who hope to attract attention (e.g., YouTube) might support their users by providing recommendations on how to attract a large public. This begins by providing examples or support in the tagging of online contents or explaining how certain elements attract attention.

Developers should also take greater responsibility in supporting their users in the communication skill of creating an online profile. Profile creation is especially relevant in social networking. Providers of such sites should ensure that people create profiles in a responsible manner. Currently, it seems that SNS primarily encourage people to reveal as much personal information as possible. People should be made aware of possible privacy concerns. They might, for example, be asked to limit the range of people who can read their posts. Before publishing online profiles, people might be asked to question what they might lose when going public. Many people seem to be sloppy about online privacy; therefore, it is advisable for SNS to ask their users to think carefully before posting private profile information.

It seems that few sites ensure that their users carefully consider what they include in their profiles. The only exception may be online dating services.

A final recommendation might be sought in the fact that people compensate a skill's shortage with another skill (Van Deursen et al., 2014). For example, when an individual lacks information skills, he or she might ask for help. Suppliers can anticipate such situations. For example, with Yahoo! Answers, people both ask and answer questions. Furthermore, users actively participate in regulation because they have the option to vote for users' answers, mark interesting questions, or report abusive behavior. Such examples of supported collective intelligence might be beneficial for people who lack either information skills or communication skills.

Improving Content from a Content Creation Skill Perspective

Content can be not only written texts such as articles, blog posts, reviews, and so on, but also photos, videos, songs, and so on. In our view, education is important in teaching people to design and create contents that are effective in communicating the correct information to the intended audience. However, how can developers encourage people to create content of higher quality? Many guidelines on how to create content are available, including recommendations for people who have not yet done so. There are tools to virtually help individuals create any content, from websites, weblogs, bulletin boards, books, ecards, tutorials, music clips, to complete movies. Often, tools are specifically designed for one type of content and provide several recommendations during the design process. In most cases, however, these tools focus on limiting the technical knowledge needed. As previously discussed, this does not automatically result in high textual quality, clear messages or purposes, or an understandable creation. The quality of the content, however, determines the success of the creation and interest among the target audience. From a supply point of view, in addition to supporting the technical process in content creation, tool developers might attempt to make their users more aware of the clarity of their creation. For example, developers could ask creators to check whether what they wrote or designed was created with the intended audience's needs and interests in mind. They might also ask their users to consult with others before posting the creation.

Improving Content from a Strategic Skill Perspective

Very unequally divided parts of the population benefit from Internet use. As demonstrated in the chapter 3, to benefit from the Internet or obtain positive effects of Internet use, a high level of strategic skills is required.

Unfortunately, most people lack the skills to benefit from Internet use. Furthermore, accounting for lower levels of strategic skills is a difficult challenge for Web developers. The suggestions outlined in the prior sections support individuals in their strategic uses of the Internet. Strategic skills involve decision-making about various issues such as health, wealth, family, and politics. For relatively simple choices in decision-making a growing number of decision support applications are offered, such as price comparison sites, voting guides, and product type choice lists. However, for general questions of information in more complex strategic choices very little aids are available.

The performance tests revealed that most Internet users do not perform the final step in the more complicated decision-making process, namely, making a decision based on a complete set of necessary pieces of information gathered online. The first step in the process seems to be difficult; problem orientation is difficult because the Internet offers many distractions. Overcrowded and abruptly changing multimedia screens create an overwhelming environment. The second step involves taking the correct actions, for example, consulting the correct sources and combining and comparing information from these sources. This step is also difficult because the number of possible actions is quite large. Although there are many choices, most people visit only one site and make a decision based on one incomplete piece of information. Nonetheless, it is difficult to determine which information source to choose, as shown in prior sections. Strategic skills involve the selection and comparison of various information sources to make a decision. Although people often base their choice on a single piece of information (when many more viewpoints are required), they seem to be convinced that their choice is correct. In the chapter 3, we illustrated that the possession of higher levels of strategic skills is necessary to gain most of the positive effects of Internet use (of note, these were all perceived effects, which do not necessarily indicate that people made the correct choice or experienced such effects regularly). We have observed that the level of strategic skills strongly relates to an individual's educational attainment level. However, developers can provide assistance to those with lower levels.

In business environments, much has been written on decision-making support systems (DSS). Beyond the business context, DSS are increasingly developed for individuals' everyday choices. DSS provide users with an easy-to-understand process for organizing their thinking. To help Internet users maintain a strong focus, perform the correct actions, and make the correct choices, DSS that address daily life decisions are becoming even more popular. There are several examples of such online systems. Unfortunately, these systems often have a strong—hidden—commercial drive. For example,

DSS that help people select a mobile phone subscription might as well be biased toward the mobile phone agencies, although not specifically mentioned. Furthermore, several independent systems only receive returns on their investments based on the number of visitors who use the system. DSS appear to be quite helpful to a large number of users and can be developed for several choices that people face, for example, national voting guides that support people in their choice of politicians or political parties. DSS limit distraction and automate several steps that many Internet users are not capable of completing alone. The diffusion of web-based services pushed the development of DSS for a large variety of applications, for example, selecting a mobile phone subscription, a specific healthcare institution, an affordable and reliable Internet service provider, a holiday agency, or a bank with the highest interest rates, to name a few. To overcome commercial influences on the decision-making process, DSS might be employed with a quality hallmark that indicates the degree of independence and reliability.

Users must also be informed of the limitations of these systems. In most cases, it is not advisable to blindly follow the provided suggestions. DSS typically make automated decisions based on user input. In the current environment, however, a new wave of DSS is developing, following the increasing amount of available social networks. When DSS incorporate user group decision-making, the suggestions and subsequent benefits are not solely provided by an automated piece of software, but also by the knowledge of others. SNS provide a valuable infrastructure for collective intelligence that might be used to gain individual benefits. Group decision-making differs from personal decision-making in that decisions are based on choices that other individuals made and evaluated. This learning-from-others allows users to determine the choices that others considered, their objectives, and the most valuable aspects of each choice. The choices that people make can be incorporated in DSS and used as a reference by similar others. Ideally, users are offered the opportunity to choose with whom, how, and when they interact with relevant stakeholders such as political parties, financial advisors, mortgage brokers, or medical experts when undergoing the decision-making process.

Conclusions

Digital skills are a complex policy problem that calls for both technological and educational solutions. In this chapter, technological supply-oriented solutions are proposed, with a focus on Internet services. Improvements in interface development can be derived from a medium-related skills perspective. Experienced operational and formal skill-related problems indicate several recommendations that developers might consider. When designing new services and applications, designers too often seem to focus primarily on creating an attractive design rather than an accessible or user-friendly design. Because information and services are often offered online with the expectation that all individuals are able to use them, this trend is worrisome. One approach discussed in this chapter is User-Centered Design, which forces designers to test their personal beliefs about how people use their creations. Furthermore, specific attention should be paid to services on mobile devices. Although the stress on operational and formal skills is relieved by providing a more intuitively preprogrammed use, it becomes increasingly difficult to employ one's content-related skills on such devices. The main reason for this difficulty is that the relatively easy and intuitive use of these media promotes a more consumptive, instead of productive and creative, use. We believe the shift toward mobile devices might even accelerate the usage gap discussed in chapter 3.

Difficulties in information, communication, content creation, and strategic Internet skills also indicate several improvements regarding how users might be supported in their quest to gain from the Internet. The levels of these skills in general appeared to be quite low. Unfortunately, developers' insufficient anticipation of lower levels seems to worsen the problem. From an *information* skills perspective, we believe that improvements in online information provision would benefit many users, especially those with lower and intermediate levels of education. This chapter provided several insights on how the functionality of existing search systems and information provision in general can be improved. These insights are derived from the information-seeking process. For example, it is suggested that public initiatives should focus on identifying the specific services that different segments of the population need and/or are interested in. This goes beyond the often-applied quantitative approach that results in an excessive amount of information and services for Internet users who already struggle with the plentitude of available information. The *communication* Internet skill perspective also suggests several recommendations for improvement. For example, we suggest that developers should take greater responsibility in supporting their users regarding the communication skill of creating an online profile. Currently, it seems that many social networking sites primarily encourage people to reveal as much personal information as possible. People are scarcely made aware of possible privacy concerns or asked to limit the range of people who can read their posts. From a *content creation* skill perspective, in addition to supporting the technical process in content creation, tool developers might attempt to make their users more aware of the clarity of their creation. For example, developers could ask creators to check whether what they wrote or designed was created with the intended audience's needs and interests in mind. Finally, from a *strategic* skill perspective, developers might further support the development of decision support systems. To help Internet users maintain a strong focus, perform the correct actions, and make the correct choices, decision support systems (DSS) that address daily life decisions are becoming ever more popular. DSS appear to be quite helpful to a large number of users and can be developed for several choices that people face.

Further Reading

- The World Wide Web Consortium (W3C)—W3C.org
  International community that develops open web standards to ensure the long-term growth of the Web.
- Schneiderman, B., & Plaisant, C. (2010). *Designing the user interface: Strategies for effective human-computer interaction.* Berkeley, CA: Pearson Education.
  Principles and guidelines to develop high-quality interface designs, based on theoretical foundations.
- Garret, J. J. (2010). *The elements of user experience. User centered design for the web and beyond.* Berkeley, CA: Pearson Education.
  Reference for web and interaction designers that goes beyond the desktop to include information that also applies to mobile devices and applications.

CHAPTER 6

Solutions: Learning Digital Skills

Introduction: How People Develop Digital Skills

The second way to overcome digital skill divides is the first to come to mind. It is the education or training of users to acquire these skills. Apparently, people first consider the obligations of users, ignoring the responsibility of designers. As argued in the previous chapter, this is not justified. However, is education the solution for digital skills divides? Strikingly, some individuals do not choose formal education as a means to learn digital skills. This is shown through an inventory of the means that Internet users choose. Figure 6.1 contains this inventory for European Internet users in 2011.

This figure shows that formal education and courses for adult education only have minority support as means to learn digital skills for the (European) population at large. There is no reason to expect that this differs in other parts of the world. Self-study by doing or books and assistance from proximate people in the social environment are far more important. These ways, often called informal learning, are rising in popularity. This might be caused by the growing user-friendliness of Internet applications that leads people to believe that they can learn on their own because they are able to start working with the applications. As observed in the performance tests of Internet users, which were described in chapter 4, this impression is misleading.

Nevertheless, it is important to note that self-study and learning from the social environment are the most popular means to acquire digital skills. When they are adequate, they are the best methods because they are the most natural, motivating, fast, and convenient methods (Van Dijk, 2005). However, these solutions are often insufficient. Learning by trial and error can also be a laborious, frustrating, inefficient, and ineffective method. People tend

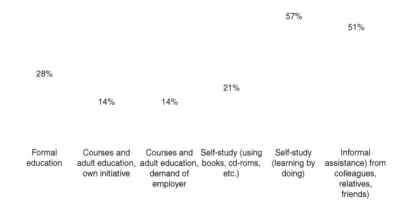

Figure 6.1 Ways of Acquiring Computer and Internet Skills.

Source: Eurostat Community Survey on ICT Usage by Households and by Individuals between 16–74 years old (2011). EU27 without Malta.

to learn and use only a fraction of the applications that could benefit them. Furthermore, some means to reach a goal can, in fact, be a detour. However, once individuals employ such a method, they continue to do so. Finally, as shown in chapter 4, people often assess their digital skill levels with so-called button knowledge as a reference point. Thus, they believe that their digital skills are adequate when they are, in fact, deficient, especially when the entire range of skills as defined in this book is considered.

To explain how digital skills can best be learned, we will begin with the most natural way to learn them, that is, learning by doing and by people in the social environment who can be asked for help. This includes parental guidance of children, who seem to spontaneously learn to use digital media from the moment that they can walk or perhaps even earlier. We will argue that formal education and adult courses remain necessary for learning appropriate digital skills. In particular, we will claim that the older generations primarily need these types of education to learn or improve the medium-related operational and formal skills, whereas the younger generations need formal education the most to learn more and better content-related information, communication, and strategic skills. This does not rule out that informal learning could help every age category in all types of digital skills.

Subsequently, we turn to formal education in schools at all levels and in training for work. Discussion of the last type of learning is continued in a special section about digital skills at work.

The final section of this chapter focuses on individuals who were not provided sufficient opportunities to learn digital skills at school or at work or who need a training update. Generally, this refers to the older portion of the population and those with jobs that did not require computers or Internet applications until fairly recently. The first opportunities to repair this lack of skills are adult and distant education. The second context is local community services such as community access centers or Internet cafés and public services such as libraries and training facilities for digital government and health services. The final section will discuss the opportunities of people who have special needs in learning digital skills, the differently abled, the elderly, the illiterates, and migrants.

Learning by Doing and via People You Know

In this section, two types of natural learning are discussed. We begin with learning by doing or self-study. Then, asking proximate others for help is discussed. As shown in figure 6.1, both types of learning are by far the most important ways to learn to use digital media.

Learning by Doing

It is no surprise that learning by doing is such an important option for dealing with skill insufficiencies. It is an age-old type of learning by direct action that fits to a so-called enactive mode of experience. This active mode differs from the relatively passive iconic and symbolic modes, which refer to learning by vision and language (Bruner & Olsen, 1973). For humans, exploring the environment and manipulating objects is a natural way to learn (Bruner, 1961). This is also called *discovery learning*, as opposed to direct instruction. However, there are advantages and disadvantages of this type of learning that appear in the context of learning digital skills.

The first advantage is that this type of learning is most rewarding, particularly when it results in success. Then, people will continue to explore and are motivated to continue using the medium concerned. The second advantage is that contemporary digital technology, especially interface design, invites people to learn in this manner. Most people immediately begin to explore the features, the applications, and menu structures of every new device that they obtain. Very few people first consult operation manuals (source). Many people consider consulting a help function as defeat. Thus, the most user-friendly technology is achieved when the hardware and software are designed in such a way that users are able to intuitively determine how they work. The technical evolution of digital media in the last 30 years supports discovery learning by users. A personal computer in the 1980s was so complicated that consulting operating manuals and taking computer courses was considered to be a necessity. Now, when people purchase a handheld computer, they immediately switch on the device and begin to explore its features, sweeping pictures, icons, and menus. The third advantage of learning by doing is that it supports our memory. Things learned in this manner stick to our minds more than things learned by direct instruction, primarily when such instruction crams things into our heads. According to Bruner (1961), people are more likely to remember concepts if they discover them on their own than if they are taught by instruction.

Unfortunately, learning by doing also has a number of important disadvantages that may urge people to also engage in other types of learning. The first problem is that learning by doing may not only be rewarding but also frustrating. The ability to find the correct direction or procedure may lead to despair and termination of the application use. The second disadvantage is that learning by doing does not work when particular basic knowledge is lacking. At least, some knowledge is needed (Alfieri, Brooks, Aldrich, & Tenenbaum, 2011). The appropriate use of many digital media cannot be intuitively learned without any prior knowledge. Another problem is that learning by doing is quite opportunistic. As soon as one has found a particular solution to an experienced problem, one continues using this self-discovered solution, even when it is a detour or a third-best option. Discovery learning ends when a workable answer is found. In this way, no new operations are found and only a fraction of the tools in a particular device or program is used most of the time. The third problem is that learning by doing lacks structure. Generally, discovery learners do not discover problem-solving rules (Mayer, 2004). When they find a way, they do not know *why* it works (the rule). After some time, they forget how they previously found the answer to a problem. Thus, they are not able to repeat the solution. When this occurs, one of the main advantages of learning by doing, better remembrance, is cancelled out. One of the reasons is that discovery learning creates a high *working* memory load that is harmful for simultaneous learning based on long-term memory (Kirschner, Sweller, & Clark, 2006).

When comparing the advantages and disadvantages of learning by doing, we conclude that this option to develop digital skills works best when it is combined with suitable types of instruction in the shape of guidance, training, or courses supported by learning tools.

Asking Proximate Others for Help

The second natural way to learn digital skills is to ask proximate others for help. Figure 6.1 shows that this is the second most important way of acquiring computer and Internet skills. People learn digital skills in particular social contexts assisted by individuals who they relate to in these contexts. These contexts depend on their current life phase. "People accumulate skills over the life course—building on and sometimes losing previously learned competencies—with their ability to use a computer intrinsically linked with what they are using a computer for at the present. In this respect, individuals live technological careers mediated by local contexts of individual and shared technology use" (Selwyn, 2005, p. 132). The home is the most relevant context for small children, and the workplace is the most relevant context for people after school age. It is less obvious that this is the case for all others in developed societies. In developed countries, the home and the workplace (not schools or training centers), are the most important places where digital skills are learned (Selwyn, 2005). This is especially true for countries with high household Internet connectivity and with most jobs requiring these skills. In developing societies, schools and local communities supported by access centers, Internet cafés, and mobile phone connections are the most relevant locations (Van Dijk, 2005).

In developed societies, small children primarily learn to use computers and the Internet at home by themselves or with the help of their parents, although some research shows that young people do not talk about their Internet use with representatives of other generations (see Kalmus, 2013). As children grow up, the assistance of brothers, sisters, friends, and neighbors becomes increasingly important (De Haan & Huysmans, 2002). At school age, the home remains the most important locus for learning digital skills. In the most developed countries, nearly every household with school-aged children has a computer and an Internet connection. School might be an important place for initial computer instruction and learning via teachers, but the home is the place for practice and computer leisure and play. Here, pupils also learn and receive assistance from fellow-pupils and proximate friends.

After school age, the workplace becomes equally important as the home to be a relevant locus for learning digital skills (Selwyn, Gorard, & Furlong, 2006). Here, colleagues are the most important source for help and learning. Following the workplace, the helpdesk of an organization is the most proximate source. Outside of the work context, friends, acquaintances, and neighbors remain an important third source of help (Van Deursen & Van Dijk, 2014b).

For older generations that did not learn to use computers and the Internet at school or work, and certainly did not learn computer and Internet skills from their parents, home support and formal computer education (computer classes and books) are the most important ways to learn digital skills. At home, they learn from their spouses or partners, children or grandchildren or neighbors, and the extended family (Correa, Straubhaar, Spence, & Chen, 2012; De Haan & Huysmans, 2002; Selwyn et al., 2006).

The advantages of learning from people we know are twofold. First, assistance is close and familiar. It comes from people who are trusted by the user and who know, more or less, what the user wants. The helper and user typically understand each other's needs and speak the same type of language. The second benefit is that this type of help and potential learning is faster than the assistance of helpdesks, average help functions, and instructors. Learning from people you know is closest to the most natural way, learning by doing. Typically, it is the next step when one is stuck in a particular operation.

Learning from people you know also has a number of basic disadvantages. First, there is no guarantee that social support will be helpful. The chances are small that the helper is a professional in digital skills or has real didactical qualities. Thus, the advice provided might not be adequate. It might be vague or come down to a particular trick that the helper has learned without knowing why it works, let alone being able to explain how. For example, many "digital natives" are not able to instruct their (grand)parents because they do not understand their parents' frame of mind in using computers and the Internet or because they act too quickly. The second disadvantage of this method of learning is that it might not work for people who most need skill improvements, for example, those who are isolated or have poor resources. People with extended social networks and a job have the best chances of support from several sources simultaneously; conversely, people with small social networks and without jobs have the least support (Van Dijk, 2005). Children of poor and low-educated families do not receive adequate support from their parents and siblings at home, whereas children of wealthy and high-educated families receive support from all sides, including parents, homework assistants, brothers and sisters, other relatives, and friends.

Learning at Work

Following the home environment, the workplace is the most important place where digital skills are learned. Learning on the job occasionally occurs when a computer or ICT training at work, or in special computer classes, is followed. In a 2012 nationally representative survey of the Dutch labor population, we asked all those working at least 12 hours per week and at least 2 hours per day with a computer for the primary source of learning ICT use at work (Van Deursen & Van Dijk, 2014b). In line with the previous paragraph, most respondents mentioned their coworkers first (38 percent), followed by the Internet and books (19 percent), and people outside of work (15 percent). Only small numbers claimed to have learned from formal organizational provisions such as ICT training (11 percent) and helpdesks (11 percent). The help function of the computer was mentioned by 5 percent.

When people at work experience serious ICT problems such as malfunctioning hardware and software and have insufficient skills to solve a particular problem, they turn to provisions that are organized by the employer. On that occasion, only a minority attempted to solve problems experienced alone (29 percent of the respondents). However, most of the respondents (48 percent) sought aid from a helpdesk or asked a coworker for assistance (18 percent). Unfortunately, they received insufficient help through this method (see below). Three percent of the respondents attempted to obtain help outside of the work environment. Malfunctioning hardware and software is a frequent and serious problem. The same survey showed that, on average, 4 percent of working time with ICTs was lost in Dutch labor organizations. An additional 3.4 percent of working time was lost on account of digital skill insufficiencies (Van Deursen & Van Dijk, 2014b).

The formal organizational solutions to problems with using ICTs at work are typically inadequate. Helpdesks serve as emergency aids that mainly provide technical assistance by repairing hardware or programming software. Typically, they do not have the didactic qualities to repair a lack of digital skills among workers. For this goal, ICT training or schooling is occasionally organized. In the above mentioned survey, only 20 percent of Dutch workers had received computer training in the last three years. Remarkably, those who seem to need these trainings most, senior and low-educated workers, attended the trainings least often. The importance of these trainings was underestimated by both management and workers. The respondents who had not attended ICT training in the past three years assessed that they would gain an average of 16 minutes of working time each day after attending such training. However, the respondents who attended ICT training reported to have gained an average of 33 minutes each day (Van Deursen & Van Dijk, 2014b).

The results of the survey among the Dutch labor force indicate that at work, management leaves people to themselves to solve digital skill-related problems. Only 22 percent declared that they learned the most from formal training and helpdesks. Rather, workers attempt to find informal solutions in solving problems such as learning by doing and asking colleagues or people outside of work. This finding also suggests that organizations do not actively monitor and stimulate the development of necessary skills. This is especially true for the individuals who most need skill training, that is, less-educated workers. Employers expect that hiring younger employees is a solution, but the survey did not observe that younger employees lost less labor time on account of skill deficiencies than older employees (Van Deursen & Van Dijk, 2014b). This might be because aging only relates to medium-related operational and formal skill problems. People of all ages require improvement in content-related skills.

Learning Digital Skills in Regular Formal Education

Pupils and students learn digital skills both at schools and outside of school, primarily at home. In terms of learning, the two environments are quite different. The skills at school are directed by teachers and the educational goals of formal curricula. The skills outside of classrooms, mainly at home, are learned by pupils or children themselves, sometimes guided by their parents. The larger part of this learning is performed in the context of entertainment and social networking, and a much smaller part is performed in the context of homework for school. Here, most operational, formal, communication, content creation, and strategic skills are learned by young people through trial and error. Many (older) teachers believe that their pupils or students have better digital skills than they do. They tend to think that they cannot educate in this area because they place digital skills on par with operational skills. Conversely, children or students feel that computers at school are an altogether different digital world than the games, chatboxes, and social media experienced outside of school (Buckingham, 2012).

We will now discuss the learning in formal education of the six skills distinguished in this book.

Operational and Formal Skills

Operational and formal skills are mainly learned in practice, outside of official educational settings (De Haan & Huysmans, 2002). In the Netherlands, in 2007, less than half of the teachers felt sufficiently confident in their digital skills to teach these skills (Kennisnet, 2007). This was mainly reported by the relatively older teachers in secondary schools, where only 50 percent used computers in classrooms, compared to primary schools, where 90 percent used computers. Primary schools regularly offer computer classes that add to the skills learned at home and in leisure time.

The situation in secondary schools as described here is unsatisfactory. Spontaneous learning outside of the classroom mainly results in learning what is urgent at a particular moment. It is likely to be partial and insufficient for many purposes, as many important operations, applications, and opportunities are bypassed. The high pace of evolution of information technology also obliges children to continually improve their skills. These skills also develop through learning by doing, trying things out, sharing one's problems, and seeing what others are doing. However, mastering the Internet and the specific operational and formal skills for particular applications also requires formal training.

The necessity of formal training becomes even more apparent when children with different family backgrounds are compared. Ba, Tally, and Tsikalas (2002) revealed that middle-income parents developed fairly advanced computer and Internet skills through their jobs and schooling and were able to show rich and varied uses. They engaged their children in critical talk about the Internet. These children appeared to have sufficient leisure time at home to develop their computer and Internet skills. They used their computers for varied purposes, ranging from work to fun and social interaction. Opposed to this, many low-income parents did not have computer experience and were less able to show what they learned to their children. Their children appeared to have less leisure time and such time was spent relatively more on the street than in their homes. They used their computer primarily for schoolwork.

Fortunately, students are increasingly encouraged to use the computer, the Internet and email for completing homework, looking up information for projects, preparing and presenting talks, and cooperative learning and communicating with classmates (e.g., Cox et al., 2004; Somekh et al., 2002). However, attention to these skills in classes is not a standard component. In primary education, there is some attention to learning operational Internet skills, especially the skills needed for word processing. In secondary education, however, many teachers tacitly assume that students know how to use the computer, surf the web, and communicate via email (Kuhlemeier & Hemker, 2007); thus, no further attention is given to these skills. In fact, the main assumption is that young people of the digital native generation possess sophisticated knowledge of and skills with information technologies (Bennett, Maton, & Kervin, 2008). However, prior to using the Internet in educational programs, tests should indicate whether students have an adequate level of operational and formal Internet skills. If not, they should first be taught these skills.

Information Skills

The situation in terms of information skills is completely different. These skills are not sufficiently learned at home, in practice or by trial and error.

These skills, adapted to the context of computers and the Internet, might also be neglected at schools when teachers and school authorities equate digital skills with operational skills and only train information skills in the context of printed media and other traditional learning materials. Information skills are not automatically learned in computer and Internet operations. Many students of secondary and even tertiary education clearly lack information skills (e.g., Kuiper, Volman, & Terwel, 2004; Van Deursen & Van Diepen, 2013).

In our performance tests, we observed that both information and strategic Internet skill levels are quite low, especially among the younger generations. In general, the search process required an excessive number of steps and a considerable amount of time. As described in chapter 4, when using search engines, people experience problems such as defining search queries, choosing search results, and failing to evaluate sources for reliability and validity. In a Dutch survey of parents and children, less than half of the parents claimed to practice these skills and their children rated themselves even lower. For example, 68 percent of children claimed to click on search result links without reading the description (Jager & Gillebaard, 2010).

Communication, Content Creation, and Strategic Skills

Communication and strategic skills are also clearly inadequate among children and pupils. Strategic skills in particular require systematic knowledge and life experience. They are a matter of lifelong learning. Currently, communication skills are only attained by practice and trial and error. Where else should children learn to email, chat, or engage in social networking? The same is true for content creation skills. People begin to create a personal website, a blog, a video, or a photograph for the web through the assistance of available software that is deceivingly easy to operate but results in amateur productions at best.

Concerning strategic skills, some attention is given in media classes or media education to issues that worry parents, teachers, and other educators. Here, issues such as being approached by strangers, pornography, teasing by fellow students, and other improper behavior on the Internet are sometimes discussed. However, media education is typically a marginal subject whose contents largely depend on the preferences of the teachers. In fact, important strategic and communication skills such as when to reveal personal information and how to distinguish public and private profiles on the Internet are not taught.

What should formal education at all levels do to help pupils or students in learning the relevant skills? Considering operational and formal Internet skills, separate classes are likely the most straightforward solution. However, information and strategic Internet skills may be better implemented in existing courses of the school curriculum. When information and strategic Internet skills are implemented in existing courses such as language, history, biology, and geography, they will be more effectively learned than when special computer classes for information skills are developed. Furthermore, teachers of regular curriculum subjects will be more motivated to spend additional time and effort on teaching these skills.

Special attention should be paid to Internet information skills. This is also true for higher education, where it cannot be expected that students have developed sufficient information and search engine use skills. It seems that standards provided, for example, by the American ACRL (Association of College and Research Libraries), tend to be quite broad rather than providing concrete directions for practical need. The first objective should be using search engines. Additional training in information skills on the Internet is highly recommended for teachers. Subsequently, they will be able to integrate these skills into their courses. It is also important to develop educational material that is appropriate for Internet use.

As argued above, communication and strategic skills can be addressed in media education classes, with special attention to legal, security, privacy, and identity issues.

Finally, a critical view on contemporary education systems as a whole is recommended. Regarding technology in education, students have been variously described as disappointed (Oblinger, 2003), dissatisfied (Levin & Arafeh, 2002), and disengaged (Prensky, 2005a). The main problem is that children and young students' experience using the Internet in their home environments and in schools is quite different. Formal education must incorporate students' Internet experience outside of school into classes. Conversely, students must incorporate the medium- and content-related skills that they learn at school into their daily Internet use. This requires more than the formal adaption of curricula. Teaching methods must be adapted to satisfy the needs of both teachers and students.

Learning in Adult and Distance Education

When people leave school and do not use computers and the Internet at work, they are left to themselves in learning digital skills. People who were approximately 40 years old in the year 2012 (approximately 20 years after the introduction of the World Wide Web) have not received the opportunity to learn these skills in school. If they did not find a job that requires computer work, this situation continues. Thus, after school age, informal means of learning by doing and with the help of the social environment, mostly at home, become increasingly important (Selwyn et al., 2006).

However, a number of people feel that they need more formal adult education to learn digital skills. Some of them turn to computer books to learn in practice. The older people are, the more they seek help in computer books (Van Dijk, De Haan, & Rijken, 2000). Others turn to computer courses that offer online or offline personal guidance. The latter is a type of formal adult education. The practice of these courses is not particularly widespread. We estimate that, on average, between 5 and 10 percent of people after school age in the developed countries have ever followed a computer course. See Selwyn et al., (2006) for UK figures and Van Deursen and Van Dijk (2014b) for Dutch statistics. In 2011, more than ten million Europeans had followed one or more modules of the European Computer Driver License (ECDL), but most of them were people with a job.

The main target group for the adult education of digital skills is seniors above 55 or 65. Unfortunately, middle-aged people between 40 and 55 are often neglected, even though many of them did not have the opportunity to learn these skills sufficiently. The digital skills problems of seniors are much more obvious. In all countries, interest and pressure groups call for computer and Internet classes for seniors. In the last section of this chapter, we will discuss the special problems of teaching digital skills to the elderly.

The vast majority of computer and Internet courses are completely focused on operational and formal skills. The modules of the International and European Computer Driver's License clearly testify to this statement. Even when the use of a search engine is included, the operational and formal skills of search tasks are taught, but the information skills required for the selection and evaluation of search results are not taught. Content-related Internet skills are mainly learned in the context of online courses on substantial topics of interest to people for their work, education, or leisure time. This refers to adult education *with* ICTs rather than adult education *about* ICTs, as discussed thus far.

Following online courses for work, study, or hobbies is more popular than following computer and Internet courses to learn digital skills. Approximately 20 percent of Internet users in the developed countries follow a particular type of online course (Eurostat Statistics, 2013). Most likely, these users learn both some content-related and medium-related skills in passing. However, the degree to which they reach a satisfactory level is unknown because learning digital skills is not an explicit goal of these courses.

Online courses in distance education have been presented as a magic solution for lifelong learning. However, 15 to 20 years of experience with distance education using ICTs shows a disillusioning picture of this type of adult education and of lifelong learning in general. A survey in the UK (England and Wales) showed that only 6 percent of an overall sample of more than one thousand British respondents reported using the Internet more than "rarely" for participating in online courses/lessons on the web, whereas 30 percent reported to have "learned something" from a computer program while using it (Selwyn et al., 2006). The number of nonparticipants to any adult education reached 37 percent; additionally, the number of transitional learners (one episode of adult education directly following compulsory education) was 18 percent, that of delayed learners (an episode of adult education later in life) was 25 percent, and that of lifelong learners was 21 percent (see Selwyn et al., 2006, Table 4.1).

Selwyn et al. found that only the transitional, delayed, and lifelong learners followed courses about or with ICT. Furthermore, they observed that lifelong learners reached the highest rates of formal and informal learning. A social-demographic analysis revealed that the same people who benefit most from all types of education also take advantage of adult education and lifelong learning and of learning with and about ICT in particular, that is, those with higher education and higher occupational class. Specifically related to ICT, young people and males were also important beneficiaries (Selwyn et al., 2006).

Selwyn et al. (2006) came to the sober conclusion that there is no reason to assume that the availability of ICT will change the situation for adults who were not previously engaged in learning and education because of a lack of motivation and social disposition. "ICTs may have little, if any beneficial impact on existing patterns of lifelong learning" (p. 34). The availability of easily accessible learning opportunities of ICT at home has not given an impetus for adult learning.

Such a disillusion should not lead to pessimism and passivity in searching for solutions for digital skills improvement in the field of adult education. There is simply no alternative for people between 40 and very old age who did not have the opportunity to previously learn these skills. Many of these people require more or less structured formal learning or informal learning of ICTs with assistance from others. It is preferable to examine the causes of insufficient interest for adult education in the field of ICT. The UK survey conducted by Selwyn et al. (2006) revealed that the main problems are a lack of motivation to use and learn ICTs, practical problems such as the time and the money needed for courses and the fact that many computer and Internet applications do not fit into the everyday life needs of potential users.

With the exception of the lack of time and money, these impediments are liable to improve. The UK survey was conducted approximately ten years ago. Since that time, computers and the Internet have completely merged into everyday life and a large number of daily activities in developed countries. In these countries, motivation is rising among ever-larger sections of the population. Even people of very high senior age want to learn to use a computer and the Internet, if only to communicate with their (grand) children.

To improve motivation, adult education courses about and with ICTs should be better adapted to the needs of particular groups. Currently, only senior and differently abled people can rely on courses that are specially tailored for them (see last section below). Most adult education of digital skills follows the same standards for all, offering modules mainly focused on operational and formal skills. Teaching higher, content-related digital skills provides the opportunity to pay greater attention to the content that interests particular groups.

Learning in Public Access Centers and Communities

In developed countries, the locus of last resort for people without home access to computers and the Internet or with a complete lack of digital skills is a particular site for public access. There are many types of such sites, ranging from Community Access Centers (CAC) or Community Technology Centers (CTC), general community centers, public libraries, publicly accessible schools, museums, hospitals, municipal halls, and churches to commercial locations such as supermarkets, service centers, and Internet cafés. However, in developing countries, public access is the first resort for people without access and skills. In these countries, home access is only available for a small minority of the population. Schools and workplaces also lack sufficient access points and training facilities. The importance of public access increases in countries with less computer and Internet access.

There is a lack of sustained empirical evidence related to the effectiveness of public access sites in terms of stimulating either ICT use or ICT-based learning (Selwyn et al., 2006). Devins, Darlow, and Smith (2002, p. 942) also conclude that there is "little evidence in the public domain associated with the learning outcomes or impact of such centers in relation to skills development, public access and in tackling issues associated with digital exclusion." This must be a disillusioning conclusion for policymakers who generally believe that these locations are the only way to reach adults who have a lack of access and skills. In developed countries, home access is the norm and the first choice of every user. Public access is the last option. "CTCs may be fixing the problem of technology access inequalities in much the same way that food banks address hunger" (Hick, 2006, p. 64).

Fortunately, this sober conclusion can be qualified, as will be explained in this section. In developed countries, public access has several important functions, although for only a small minority of the population. In supporting digital skills, its role could and should grow, as will be argued in this book. In developing countries, the role of public access centers can be rated much higher. In these countries, these centers play a vital function in providing both access and skills support.

The first function of public access sites is to provide access, mostly occasional access to computers and the Internet for those without a home, work, or school connection. The second function is incidental help for those who do not know how a particular computer or Internet operation should be performed or how a public service should be used. For example, in the United States, public libraries are often called to assist in the use of eGovernment services (Bertot, 2010). The third function is to provide complete computer and Internet courses. However, few public access centers perform this function, as it requires sustained access and these centers typically have insufficient staff capacity and competency to offer complete courses that are customized to a particular user group.

Most people in developed countries use public access centers only occasionally. This is especially true for experienced Internet users who sometimes experience broken home connections or are nearby a center. The last occasion occurs more often, as public access centers are used as wireless access spots. Some less experienced Internet users are more frequent users of public access (Selwyn et al., 2006). In the UK survey discussed above, these users included migrants and other typically deprived people. Another user group was returners to the job market and people attempting to restart a career (Selwyn et al., 2006). These users confirm that public access centers have an important function for particular sections of the population that are likely to be excluded otherwise. Especially in the United States, CTCs and public libraries are important in providing (broadband) access and skills support (Becker et al., 2011; Hick, 2006; Jaeger, Bertot, Thompson, Katz, Decoster, 2012; Servon & Nelson, 2001). A 2012 national survey of US public libraries (Bertot, McDermott, Lincoln, Real, & Peterson, 2011) showed that 82 percent of libraries practiced informal point-of-use assistance, 44 percent offered formal training classes, and 28 percent offered online training material.

In developing countries, public access centers perform a vital function for larger sections of the population. In these countries, they are sometimes called PC and Internet kiosks or Telecenters. They serve both business and educational or community needs. Kuriyan and Toyama (2007) categorize them into the following four types: (1) computer-education centers on a commercial basis providing operational skill courses for (mainly) children of wealthier parents, (2) regular Internet cafés, also commercial and offering various Internet services, (3) government service centers for various online government documents, and (4) photo shops for picture and video services.

Three observations are striking. First, in developing countries, public access centers are dominated by commercial supply, whereas in the developed countries, they are mainly subsidized by (local) government money. Rangaswami (2008) argues that it is better to subsidize the universally available Internet cafés and give them a public function, also in training digital skills. Second, in developing countries, the early adopters of ICTs, that is, young, higher educated, and relatively prosperous people, use public access sites most, whereas in the developed countries, main users are the last categories to adopt ICTs. Third, emphasis is on access, not on skills development. Educational functions and digital skill training facilities are relatively rare. They focus on particular target groups such as women, the poor, and people of lower castes, as in India, and these facilities continually experience maintenance problems (Kuriyan & Toyama, 2007).

Whereas in developing countries, public access centers have important community and social or meeting functions, in developed countries, these centers experience difficulties in offering such functions. In developed countries, users of these centers are goal directed, that is, they only come for a particular single function, primarily access or a particular question. Many people view these centers as unattractive, "alien" environments that are not adapted to their needs. People prefer home access and favor access with friends and neighbors above these centers (Selwyn et al., 2006). Public access site managers believe that they have a general function for all parts of the population; however, deeper analysis shows that customization to particular target groups of users might be better, for example, adapting services and training to particular local social, economic, and cultural needs and to the special competencies of clients.

A special public provision is offered by (local) governments that offer on-the-spot assistance in using the Internet to citizens who arrive at service desks with insufficient skills to use online government services. Sometimes this provision results in providing citizens complete computer and Internet classes to enable them to use online public or government services at home. There is much positive experience with these provisions in the Netherlands in terms of participation in the classes (www.digisterker.nl). These strongly goal-oriented and customized approaches to help people learn digital skills as soon as they need them might be a good alternative for the general provisions at public access sites.

Learning by Disadvantaged Groups: Disabled, Illiterate, Elderly and Migrant Users

In the final section of this chapter, we turn to a number of categories of people who require special treatment in learning digital skills. Typically, these individuals are disadvantaged in a socioeconomic sense, although this is not necessarily the case, for example, elderly people are not necessarily disadvantaged in this sense. All of these categories have a particular additional handicap in learning digital skills. Differently abled people have physical or mental handicaps that complicate the use of digital media. Illiterates are barely (if at all) able to read and write, making every use of a digital medium that contains text difficult, if not impossible. Elderly people have grown up with traditional media use and must become accustomed to entirely new forms of media use. Moreover, they become slow in learning and in operating hardware and software. With growing age, they increasingly experience problems of vision, hearing, motion, and mental capacities such as a reduced attention span and long-term or short-term memory. Finally, many migrants have cultural and language problems using digital media in their host countries.

These disadvantaged categories form special target groups in computer and Internet training. Experience shows that the differently abled have the most difficulties with operational and formal skills. The same is true for many elderly people. Illiterates have difficulties in reading the text of keyboards and menu tags on a screen. Furthermore, they can barely perform content-related skills. Migrants also have difficulties with these skills, as these skills often require the proficiency of English or the host country language, particularly when strategic skills are concerned.

These additional problems require the learning of supplementary material before digital skills can be learned or at the start of a particular course or training. Differently abled people must learn to use screen readers and magnifiers, spoken web contents, connected Braille readers, or other additional technical aids that compensate for their disability. Elderly people sometimes require the same aids. Most senior users must become accustomed to the operation of digital media. Illiterates must first learn to read and write better, or they should be taught to benefit from multimedia content when they begin using a computer or other digital medium. Migrants must learn the local language and/or English to successfully follow most computer and Internet courses. Typically, digital learning facilities in the migrants' language are lacking or are not adapted to their social and cultural needs.

We now discuss the four disadvantaged groups in a broader sense, beginning with *the differently abled*. Differently abled people could benefit even more from the use of a computer and the Internet than people without disabilities. However, they have less access to these digital media and fewer skills to use them (Dobransky & Hargittai, 2006). The benefits are more or less evident. Using the Internet, differently abled people can escape social isolation and the stigma that is often associated with the visibility of their handicap. In this way, they can remove disability from the forefront of interaction and receive a fair chance in communication. A second advantage of the Internet is that it offers many opportunities for specialized health information about their handicap and for becoming a member of self-help groups of people with the same disabilities. With the aid of the Internet, they can organize and receive assistance. Finally, online communication is able to compensate for problems of mobility.

The reality is that the differently abled meet a number of extra barriers for access and the development of skills. The issue most discussed is the accessibility of websites, which requires a special effort for improvement to adapt them to this user group. Currently, most websites do not use the official web guidelines (W3C). A second barrier is that the differently abled must purchase special assistive technologies that are often expensive and difficult to use. A third obstacle is that differently abled people might receive assistance and nursing but not the special help needed for using computers and the Internet. Often, they are not even informed about the possibilities for assistance. Helping these individuals obtain access and skills requires special expertise.

What is the state of affairs concerning the digital skills of people with disabilities? Recently, Van der Geest, Van der Meij, and Van Puffelen (2014) have investigated the same type of skills as elaborated in this book in a number of self-assessments and performance tests of the digital skills of differently abled people in the Netherlands. They compared young (12 to 18) and elderly (55+) differently abled individuals with visual impairment. One-quarter of these individuals used a Braille reader, and 48 percent utilized a screen reader or magnifier. In the self-assessments, the young individuals rated themselves higher than did the elderly. In the performance tests, the young were significantly better than the elderly in operational, formal, and information skills. However, in strategic skills, the elderly received much higher rates; they were better at completing forms, making decisions, and comparing various outcomes against implicit criteria. In general, the performances of these samples of differently abled people were roughly equal to our results for the Dutch population as a whole. However, the strategic skills of the visually impaired elderly were strikingly higher. An explanation might be that these people have been forced to stand up for themselves in achieving and making decisions throughout their lives.

The performance of the differently abled in this investigation can be appraised as quite high when we take into account the extra barriers of learning to use assistive technologies while learning to use computers and the Internet. Murphy, Kuber, McAllister, and Strain (2008) have made complete lists of these barriers and others that must be overcome to successfully learn these skills. First, very few courses in digital skills are offered to the differently abled. Second, there is a shortage of trainers who are familiar with assistive technologies. Additionally, few trainers know the special treatments required to train differently abled people. Finally, costs are high because training occurs on a one-to-one basis or in very small groups.

In addition to the problems caused by insufficiently realized W3C 1.0 web guidelines, differently abled learners of digital skills, primarily the visually impaired, experience many extra problems concerning operational and formal skills. They require more time and mental workload in browsing webpages. They rely more on their memory of page structures and contents and miss out on perceptual experience compared to fully sighted fellow users. In fact, they have an entirely different mental model in browsing the Internet compared to sighted users. Therefore, they also have difficulties in collaborating with sighted users on Internet tasks (Murphy et al., 2008, p. 88).

Initially, it seems to be a hopeless job to attempt to teach digital skills to *illiterates*. The ability to read and write is a prime condition for using computers and the Internet. Fortunately, these media are not only word processors but also multimedia machines that contain many audiovisual signs. Following sounds and pictures and using touchscreens enables illiterates to at least have some access to digital media. To use a vivid example: do not be surprised to observe that a large number of illiterates are able to obtain access to an adult site and find the related pictures when they want them. Fairly quickly, these individuals learn to recognize the letters p- o- r – n and find the buttons for typing a particular URL and for identifying the logos that stand for particular menu choices. Illiterates are able to learn basic operational and formal skills. However, content-related or higher Internet skills are beyond their capacity because they require the ability to read and write.

Capacities depend on the level of illiteracy, that is, complete and functional illiteracy. Complete illiterates are at the lowest level of literacy. They cannot read or write; the best that they can do is to learn to recognize particular letters or words on signs following their visual appearance. Functional illiterates are people with some ability to read and write but insufficient ability for their daily practical needs. They are not able to complete forms or read or write an email message, and they have difficulties in reading street signs, using an ATM, and reading a train schedule. There are a surprisingly large number of functional illiterates, even in developed countries. The Human Development Report 2009 (UNDP, 2009) estimated the numbers of functional illiterates between 1994 and 2003 to be 20 percent of the US population, 22 percent for the UK, and 47 percent in Italy, with Sweden assumed to have the lowest number (7.5 percent). In developed countries, complete illiterates are typically comprise less than 5 percent of the population; they mainly consist of mentally handicapped persons and migrants. However, in most developing countries, complete and functional illiterates together comprise the large majority of the population.

Regardless of their performance in using them, illiterates benefit from the development of digital multimedia. Compared to printed texts, digital media always present advantages. The combination of sounds, visuals, text, and animations helps to understand the meaning of contents. The rise of touchscreens with icons and pictures offers greater opportunities than traditional keyboards. One-click operations enable fast and automatic input of various types of content. However, every digital media use that is slightly more advanced poses insurmountable problems for illiterates.

For the reasons mentioned, many educators and policy makers consider teaching digital skills to illiterates to be impossible. These individuals are expected to learn to read and write first. Research on the level of digital skills among illiterates is completely absent. Literate people typically do not understand the problems and mental makeup of illiterate people (Selwyn, 2003). Sometimes, the illiterates are called the "information poor." Yu (2010) emphasizes that the "information poor" are not only deprived in a socioeconomic sense. Their lack of information search and retrieval should primarily be understood in cultural, cognitive, and behavioral terms. They often do not have the motivation to actively search for information and take the initiative to obtain access to a digital information medium. Formal information search and retrieval is not in their daily routine. They are "disadvantaged by their own information practices, which features notably the following characteristics: limited in range and variety, largely performed involuntarily while engaging in non-information practices, mostly confined to home or work places in local areas, sporadically conducted in between non-information activities, involving simple skills and superficial information processing" (Yu, 2010, p. 929).

Despite these limitations, teaching digital skills to complete and functional illiterates is not impossible. Consider that the opposite conclusion would make the job of teaching digital skills to people in developing countries an impossible mission. The training of digital skills to this target group should realize the following conditions. First, digital skills learning should occur simultaneously with literacy training, naturalization or citizenship courses, and other education that the illiterates or the information poor consider relevant. Such learning is effective and goes en passant. Second, digital skills instruction should fully benefit from the multimedia features of digital media and not immediately focus on text. Third, courses should always be tailored to the special needs of the people concerned, for example, the requirements of immigration and the need to survive in an information society (Bridge IT Thematic Network, 2010).

Another category that might benefit from using the Internet, but has less access and skills to use this medium is *the elderly*, that is, seniors aged 55 and higher. The Internet is able to compensate for declining mobility and social isolation. It is an excellent medium for the specialized information and support that the elderly need such as health information and care. It helps them to stay in touch with their (grand)children and other family members. However, across the world, surveys have shown that the elderly are the last to adopt computers and the Internet and that they have fewer digital skills than younger people. Our research reveals that they primarily display inferior operational and formal skills. However, when the elderly have these skills, they might demonstrate better information and strategic skills than younger people, taking advantage of their knowledge and experience in life (Van Deursen, 2010; Van Deursen et al., 2011).

Contrary to the lack of concern for the digital skills of illiterate and disabled people, the lag of digital access and skills among the elderly has drawn the immediate attention of societies everywhere. It is evident that they are not the so-called "digital natives" and that they must exert effort to change traditional into digital media use. As the digital media have different formal structures and require new commands to use them, it is not surprising that the elderly display inferior operational and formal skills. However, this is not the only problem that senior users face when they use digital media. Previously, we mentioned the physical and mental deficiencies many elderly experience; fortunately, not all individuals experience these deficiencies when they grow older. Aging is associated with physical declines in mobility (required to handle and carry equipment), motor skills (needed to operate a keyboard and a mouse), and vision or hearing (to perceive multimedia). To compensate for these declines, the elderly can use the same types of assistive technologies as the differently abled. Mental deficiencies include cognitive slowing and reduced attention spans or impaired short- and long-term memory (Bean, 2003).

Despite these impediments, the elderly are well able to use computers and the Internet (Czaja, 1997; Wandke, Sengpiel, M., & Sönksen, 2012). Moreover, typically, motivation is not lacking. As the digital media become more prominent in society, the motivation of even very old people to obtain access and learn the requisite skills increases. However, they "will not be interested in learning to use a computer until they experience a relevant purpose for it, and they will learn only what is of immediate use to them, such as how to view an e-mail attachment" (Bean, 2003, p. 3).

In the last 25 years, much effort has been spent in attempting to teach seniors the digital skills that they need. This teaching has been performed by institutions of adult education, public libraries, and community centers. Self-organization in the form of senior-web's or -net's organizing courses, and forms of assistance is available in nearly every country. However, with the exception of self-organization, these efforts are not sufficiently customized to elderly people. The elderly are offered the same type of courses as younger adults, and some courses are taught by young teachers. In general, "digital natives" should not provide computer classes to seniors. These younger individuals cannot imagine older adults' problems in not grasping the workings of digital technology and often perform teaching operations at a quick speed. Age-specific training that is customized to the needs and abilities of the elderly is a necessity (Bean, 2003; Rogers & Fisk, 2000; Wandke et al., 2012).

Every course or training for *seniors* should be customized to take into account the following conditions (for a complete list, see Bean, 2003; Wandke et al., 2012):

- *Relevance* to the daily life of elderly people to maintain motivation.
- Adjusted *speed of learning:* "older people require more time to process new information, more practice time to learn new tasks and consequently more training time"(Bean, 2003, p. 5).
- Consider the *mind-set* of the elderly that was created in their youth when they learned to use traditional media. The training should take into account that thinking in terms of hyperlinks and even menus may be new to the elderly. Additionally, the existing *learning style* of the individual senior should be screened and used as much as possible.
- Use of the type of *instructional material* that elderly want. Many seniors enjoy printed instructions that they can follow at their own speed. However, "using simple, clear language with illustrations or animation in instructional material works much better for older adults than lengthier, explanatory text" (Bean, 2003, p. 4).
- *Physical and mental deficiencies* should be accepted and meliorated with technical aids that are used by comparable categories of the differently abled.

- All training and courses should be adapted to the *local culture*. In traditional cultures young teachers should not be used. In some cases, for example, Islamic cultures, female teachers should not be employed for male seniors. Kim and Merriam (2010, p. 452) have observed that in South Korea, it is important to create an atmosphere in computer classes where older students can "save face" when they make mistakes. The positive and negative aspects of social and cultural interactions in computer classes should be taken into account (Kim & Merriam, 2010).

The needs of *migrants* in learning digital skills can be best compared with those of illiterates. However, this is not true for all migrants, for example, highly educated students and professionals studying and working abroad typically have a high level of digital skills. All migrants receive a large number of benefits though using computers and the Internet. ICTs can help to integrate migrants into their host country and simultaneously aid in maintaining contact with their home country and fellow migrants from the same culture in their country of destination. On the Internet, they can find relevant and practical information. ICTs are often used for obligatory immigration courses and finding jobs or training for a job. Computers are even used to teach many migrants who came to developed countries as illiterates to read and write.

Although the benefits are high, access to computers and the Internet and presumably digital skills are at a low level among poor and low-educated migrants. Unfortunately, there are no self-assessments or performance tests of the digital skills of migrants in developed countries. Most likely, differences between the original nationalities of migrants are large. For example, in the United States (where ethnic origin is an important variable in social surveys), ethnic minorities reveal substantial differences in access to computers and the Internet. In general, Asian Americans have much more access to and interest in ICT than Latino and Native Americans (see several Pew Internet and American Life surveys of the last ten years). This is not only a socioeconomic but also a cultural phenomenon.

The main problems that migrants experience in acquiring digital skills are not only low education, illiteracy, and poverty but also language problems, that is, commanding the language of the host country or English, which is the dominant language in the computer world. Further, they lack sufficient knowledge of the host culture that has shaped the local Internet applications according to its own taste and interest. Thus, this medium is not attractive to most migrants.

As with all disadvantaged groups discussed in this section, digital skills training and courses should be customized, particularly with respect to the language and culture of the ethnic group concerned. Topics and examples in courses should be relevant issues to this group, for example, passing an immigration exam and finding housing or a job. They should amply use the multimedia characteristics of ICTs that are especially important for children and illiterates, such as visuals and animations (Redecker, Haché, & Centeno, 2010). All learning materials should be translated. A main target is to learn the host language on the basis of one's mother language. In this way, the training should increasingly focus on the culture and language of arrival and on opportunities to find formal education and a job.

Conclusions

This chapter showed that formal education and courses for adult education represent only minor support as means to learn digital skills. Informal learning (self-study and assistance by people nearby) is more important. This type of learning is supported by the growing user-friendliness of Internet applications and handheld devices. Informal learning is a natural, motivating, fast, and convenient way to learn. However, many digital media cannot be intuitively learned without any prior knowledge. Another problem is that learning by doing is quite opportunistic. Informal learning to develop digital skills works best when it is combined with suitable types of instruction in the form of guidance, training, or courses. For older generations that did not learn to use computers and the Internet at school or work, home support and formal computer education (computer classes and books) are the most important ways of learning digital skills.

After the home environment, the workplace is the most important space where digital skills are learned. Here, the natural way to learn digital skills is to ask others in close proximity for help, with coworkers representing the first choice. The formal organizational solutions to problems with using ICTs at work are typically inadequate. Helpdesks serve as emergency aids that mainly provide technical assistance. ICT training or schooling is only occasionally organized. The importance of training is underestimated by both management and workers. However, research shows that employees attending ICT training could gain as much as half an hour a day of working time.

Pupils and students learn digital skills both at school and outside of school, primarily at home. In terms of learning, the two environments are quite different. The skills at school are directed by teachers and the educational goals of formal curricula. The skills outside of classrooms, mainly at home, are learned by the pupils or children themselves, sometimes guided by their parents. Operational and formal skills are mainly learned via practice, outside of official educational settings. With regard to information skills, the situation is completely different. These skills are not sufficiently learned at home, through practice or by trial and error. They may be better implemented in existing courses of the school curriculum instead of in separate classes. Communication and strategic skills can be addressed in media education classes.

In the practice of adult education, course motivation is vital. Such motivation is supported by better adapting these courses to the needs of particular groups, such as minorities, people with low education, and those who are older. Here, public access centers are helpful too, particularly in developing countries. These centers have a crucial function in providing both access and skills support.

In the final section of this chapter, a number of categories of people who require special treatment in learning digital skills were discussed: differently abled, illiterate, elderly, and migrant users. All of these categories of people have a particular additional handicap in learning digital skills. Sometimes, individuals need supplementary tools; the differently abled represent one example. Unfortunately, few trainers know the special tools and methods required to train differently abled, illiterate, elderly, and migrant people. Digital skills training and courses should be customized for all of the disadvantaged groups discussed in this section. Taking into account the special needs, handicaps, tools, and teaching methods required by all these groups can facilitate digital skills education, even for complete and functional illiterates.

Further Reading

- Bruner, J. S. (1961). The act of discovery. *Harvard Educational Review, 31*(1), 21–32.
  Classical book about formal and informal learning to be applied to contemporary learning digital skills.
- Van Deursen, A., Courtois, C., & Van Dijk, J. (2014). Internet skills, sources of support and benefiting from Internet use. *International Journal of Human-Computer Interaction.* DOI:10.1080/10447318.2013.858458.
  Empirical study about social sources of support people use to solve problems of Internet use.
- Selwyn, N., Gorard, S., & Furlong, J. (2006). *Adult learning in the digital age: Information technology and the learning society.* London and New York: Routledge.

Complete study of adult learning in learning digital skills with strong emphasis for social and cultural contexts and problems.

- Van Deursen, A., & Van Dijk, J. (2014). Loss of labor time due to skill insufficiencies and malfunctioning ICT. *International Journal of Manpower, 35*(5), in press.
Empirical study about digital skills at work, consequences of inadequacies, and their solutions.

- Buckingham, D. (2012). *Beyond technology: Children's learning in the age of digital culture.* Cambridge: Polity.
About the children learning digital skills inside and outside school in a social and cultural context (beyond technology).

- Wandke, H., Sengpiel, M., & Sönksen, M. (2012). Myths about older people's use of information and communication technology. *Gerontology, 58*(6), 564–570.
About the elderly learning digital skills, myths, and realities, and to solve problems.

CHAPTER 7

Conclusions and
Policy Perspectives

Conclusions

Digital Skills as the Key to New Media Use

This book has shown that the command of digital skills is the most crucial factor in the process of the appropriation of new information and communication technologies. When these skills are inadequate or absent, new media cannot be satisfactorily or effectively used. Motivation may be the main driver in this process of appropriation and physical access may be the main condition, but digital skills are the key to new media use. Focusing on Internet skills, we demonstrated that better Internet skills lead to longer and more diverse Internet use and that people who command these skills receive greater benefits from this medium. By contrast, we did not confirm the opinion that more Internet experience leads to better skills, at least not in regard to content-related skills. Experience only modestly improves the medium-related operational and formal skills.

The emphasis on the importance of digital skills is part of a perspective that refers to the second-level digital divide. The first level of the digital divide concentrates on access to digital technology. The second-level divide focuses on gaps in skills and usage. The effects of these gaps in terms of social and information inequality might be more profound and lasting than the relatively simple and temporary problems posed by physical access gaps. The effects of gaps in skills might cause structural inequality between classes or categories of people. These effects might produce an information elite that commands high levels of digital skills and frequent and diverse use of digital media, with much attention to applications that support work, career, and study. In addition, these effects might create groups of largely excluded people with no or very few skills, infrequent digital media use, and a preference for entertainment and leisure applications. The majority of the population may develop modest levels of skills and an interest in both so-called serious and entertainment or leisure applications. This potential dark perspective of a tripartite information and network society is outlined by Van Dijk (1999, 2012, and 2005).

The Concept of Digital Skills

Throughout this book, we have preferred the term "digital skills" to terms that contain the word "literacy", as the latter have connotations of reading and writing texts and cognitive processes. The term is derived from a former phase in media history. The use of interactive digital media includes much more than reading, writing, and understanding; it implies activities such as interactions with programs and other people, transactions in goods and services, and continually making decisions. The term "skills" seems more appropriate for this broad set of activities than the term "literacy". In addition, "skills" is preferred to the term "competency", as competency indicates a potential rather than a capacity that is utilized.

This broad concept of digital skills inspires a multidisciplinary approach. In this book, this concept has included aspects of media and communication studies, computer and technology science, educational science, information science, and a mixture of sociology and psychology. All of these disciplines are needed to analyze the many abilities that people must have to learn to use the digital media.

This is not to say that there is an absolute difference between digital skills and traditional media skills. In chapter 1, we discussed many similarities and overlap. Using the digital media requires reading and writing texts and the skills to operate, perceive, and create products of audiovisual media. However, digital media require additional skills derived from the complex and multifunctional technical, informational, interactive, and creative nature of most contemporary digital media. In this book, these skills have been called content-related skills and (mainly) applied to Internet use. Comparable skills are needed in the traditional media. However, in the digital media, they are significantly broader and more demanding. Additionally, it is assumed that the operational and formal skills of digital media are commanded.

A Framework

In chapters 1 and 2, we have proposed and developed a conceptual framework of digital skills that subsequently has been applied in empirical research using laboratory performance tests and survey self-assessments. We have made a distinction between the following six digital skills: operational, formal, information, communication, content creation, and strategic. This framework has three basic characteristics.

1. A distinction is made between *medium-related and content-related skills*. Medium-related skills differ in digital media compared to other media, whereas content-related digital media skills have many similarities with skills required to use traditional media. However, in the context of content-related skills for digital media, it is assumed that not only traditional medium-related skills such as the ability to read and write, but also the special media-related skills of digital media operation and formal structure are mastered. We have attempted to make a careful analytical distinction between these skills to investigate them in a reliable manner.

2. The distinction has a *sequential and conditional nature*. The six skills are sequential, and it is assumed that the preceding skill is mastered before the following skill can be learned to a satisfactory degree. In general, the medium-related skills precede the content-related skills.

3. The framework contains *both technical and substantive skills*. Operational and formal skills are mainly technical, whereas the other four skills are primarily substantive because they require knowledge, creativity, and particular goals or norms needed for decisions. This differs from common sense understandings of digital skills that narrow this concept to indicate the command of technical operations only. Therefore, although the term "skills" has the connotation of being instrumental, digital skills also comprise the creation and understanding of content.

The framework is limited to the basic skills that individuals need to use the digital media in a manner that is satisfactory for users. It does not contain advanced skills such as software programming, professional editing, or Internet applications that are intended for a minority of users.

The focus on basic skills also indicates that the framework does not have a preconceived normative character. This is a conspicuous characteristic of many conceptions of media literacy. Users should be "critical" media users who are able to detect the backgrounds and the public or private interests of media or content producers and who understand that they are manipulated in a particular way. In the framework developed in this book, we have attempted to be as objective and restrictive as possible. Therefore, observations of various types of digital media usage were conducted. These observations indicated which skills were needed to fully benefit from the medium and which skills were not. For example, in regard to information skills, users must identify the source of the results of search engines to compare the potential goals of the source in producing the information. When this is accomplished, search engines are used in a way that is satisfactory for users. Users do not need to learn that the goals of particular content producers are good or bad according to a particular view of the media and society.

Elaborating on the framework throughout the chapters of this book, we have clearly focused on Internet skills for two main reasons. First, the Internet is the most versatile digital medium that enables us to unfold the full scale of digital skills. Second, all other digital media are increasingly converging into or connected to the Internet. It should be fairly easy for others to extend and complete the list of six skills for other digital media such as smartphones, ereaders, digital televisions, and digital video cameras. The tables in chapter 1 initiate such extensions.

Empirical Evidence

After proposing a framework of digital skills, it is necessary to demonstrate its value and test it. Innumerable conceptual frameworks for digital literacy or skills have been developed that have not been empirically supported. At the time of writing, we have empirically tested four of the six skills in laboratory performance tests in a cross-section sample of the Dutch population, and we are planning to test the two other skills (communication and content creation skills). Additionally, we have reported the results of self-assessments of all six skills in nationwide Dutch surveys. We have attempted to collect and present the available empirical evidence of digital skills investigations across the world. After all, the results of skills research in a rich and high-access country such as the Netherlands are not representative for other countries.

In gathering evidence about the current levels of digital skills in other countries, we observed that empirical evidence is scarce and that a large part of the available evidence is gathered with doubtful methods in terms of validity and reliability. Three basic empirical methods have been employed to investigate the level of digital literacy or skills:

1. Surveys with questions that ask for the use of digital media or Internet applications, which are assumed to deliver *indirect evidence* for the command of skills. When an individual uses an application that is conceived to be difficult to use, this is held to be an indication of a high level of skills.
2. Surveys with questions that request *self-assessments* of skills. This is the most commonly used method.
3. *Performance tests* in a laboratory or other controlled environments that provide subjects with particular assignments to observe their command of skills.

We have argued that the last method is the most valid. Indirect measures register the usage of applications; however, there is no guarantee that these applications are sufficiently mastered. Self-assessments lead to the overrating and underrating of the skills possessed. We have attempted to create so-called *proxy questions* for surveys that best reflect the skills that we have distinguished. These questions were derived from the performance tests. However, it proved to be difficult to identify valid and reliable proxy questions for the content-related skills (Van Deursen, Van Dijk, & Peters, 2012). Although we prefer performance tests, we have taken an opportunistic attitude in referring to all types of evidence for current levels of digital skills worldwide. Empirical research in this field is only beginning and there is much need for improvement.

What are the main conclusions from the available empirical evidence on current levels of digital skills? The most important conclusion is that levels of medium-related skills (in the current framework, operational and formal skills) are higher than levels of content-related skills (in the current framework, information, communication, content creation, and strategic skills). Most people more or less command the operational skills needed to use the digital media, particularly the Internet. According to many observers, the problem lies in the information skills. We add communication and content creation skills to this list of problems, as they are relatively new opportunities or requirements for digital media use. However, strategic skills applied to Internet use appear to be the least mastered of all skills. Thus, many people experience difficulties in achieving their goals on the Internet when these goals require autonomous search for particular means or options on the web from several sources rather than making choices from preprogrammed menus.

The second most important conclusion is that people who have insufficient levels of medium-related skills are not able to command the higher-level content-related skills. However, sufficient medium-related skills do not guarantee that content-related skills will be mastered. This is the explanation for the current finding, perhaps surprising for many readers, that middle-aged and elderly people outperform the "digital native" young generation on information and strategic digital skills, provided that they have sufficient basic knowledge of medium-related digital skills. We have attempted to explain this finding with reference to the knowledge, level of literacy, and practical or life experience that these older generations have compared to the youngest generation. A related observation is that experience with digital media such as the Internet does not seem to improve digital skill levels, except for the medium-related skills.

Other empirical evidence of current skill levels concentrates on the demographics of skill scores. Nearly every investigation demonstrates that age and educational background are the most important variables related to skill inequalities. As age increases, digital skill levels decrease, with the exception of information and strategic skills (on the condition that operational and formal skills are commanded). Level of education attained is an even stronger correlate in the sense that it applies to all ages. People with high education score highest on every performance test.

Few gender differences in the command of digital skills are observed in developed countries that are marked by a relatively high level of gender equality. Women only show a lower level of digital media experience and skills in traditional cultures and developing countries with fewer socioeconomic opportunities. At times, skill inequalities among different ethnic groups are observed. For example, in the United States, people with Hispanic, Native, or African American background exhibit lower levels of digital skills than Americans with an Asian or Anglo-Saxon background. This result seems to be related to socioeconomic inequalities and cultural preferences.

The Problem: Exclusion

These demographic backgrounds of skill inequalities support the conclusion that these inequalities are a reflection of general inequalities in societies. Yet, we have shown that this conclusion is overly simple. Indeed, the same types of social and information inequalities appear for digital and traditional media skills. However, the main difference is that technology raises additional barriers. This barrier is harmful when people from older generations are not able to benefit from their knowledge or practical and life experience in the context of digital media use because they have insufficient operational and formal skills. It is also effective for the differently abled and elderly people with physical and mental deficiencies. Finally, it is an extra handicap for those who might be interested in digital information, culture, and particular applications but have no technical fondness or competence.

The main impact of inequalities of digital skills is more or less participation or exclusion in several fields of society. Thus, digital skills are the key to the information society. We have shown that the ability or competence of digital media use offers real benefits in economic participation (jobs, careers, wages, income, and lower prices), educational participation (school enrollment and performance, special training and courses), and political participation (voter and decision-making participation, opportunities for political information retrieval and discussion). Additionally, benefits can be expected in social participation (social contact, civic engagement, sense of community, and membership of associations), cultural participation (access to leisure and entertainment applications on the Internet, electronic reservations for cultural events, and opportunities to contribute to user-generated content on the web), and spatial participation (increasing mobility and flexibility by means of digital media to be more effective in daily life). Finally, in regard to institutional participation, people with appropriate digital skills have access to more and better publicly provided social and health benefits.

Most of the benefits listed in the previous paragraph can be received using traditional media; however, this is becoming increasingly difficult. In high-access countries, many traditional media channels are closed or made unattractive by the special effort required to use them. This refers to absolute exclusion, but relative exclusion is also effective in the long run. Such exclusion indicates that people who are quite skillful in using digital media benefit much more than those with less skill. They push aside the others in obtaining jobs, careers, powerful positions, valuable products and services, and other opportunities. They can even defeat rivals for friendships or sexual and marital relationships on social networking and online dating sites.

This increasing relative inequality reinforces existing structural inequality in all fields or spheres of society. According to the theoretical model explained in chapter 3, more or less participation in the fields or spheres of society relates to more or less resources and positions obtained in society. In this way, a cycle is created that tends to produce growing inequality in the information and network society.

Solutions

To break this cycle, a number of strategic interventions are needed. Some of the interventions are specifically focused on mitigating the information inequality that is caused by different levels of digital skills. Others are more general and aim to reduce the socioeconomic and cultural inequality that shapes the context of digital media use. This book emphasizes interventions that focus on the mitigation of information inequality by improving digital skills. However, we have also continually stressed the importance of the social, economic, and cultural contexts of digital skills. People who have no job that contains computer work, no school to attend, no school-going children at home, no money to buy a computer or other digital equipment and pay for an Internet connection, no command of the majority language or English, and no home are in a poor position to obtain digital skills. Many of these conditions are true for the vast majority of people in developing countries. Overall, giving people a job might be a better solution to the digital skills problem than giving them a computer or Internet course.

In chapters 5 and 6, we have concentrated on the specific solutions for the problem of the inequality of digital skills. These solutions are either a type of prevention through improvement of the interface design and provided content in digital media or intervention through user education.

Improvements in the accessibility and usability of digital media interface design can reduce the demands set on users in terms of medium-related skills. Designers should pay specific attention to users with lower levels of operational and formal Internet skills. Often, the main focus is creating an attractive design rather than an accessible or user-friendly design. Several consortiums offer handbooks and guidelines that designers can use. A common belief of most consortiums is that designers should take a User Centered Design approach. By employing this approach, designers are forced to test their personal beliefs concerning how others will use their creations. We also claimed that consistency in the applications offered might greatly benefit people with lower levels of operational and formal skills, who must learn things anew with every website or application. Therefore, official organizations might seriously consider the option to employ two different websites, an advanced version that accounts for the needs of Internet users with relatively difficult questions and high levels of skills and a simple version that accounts for the needs of Internet users with relatively easy questions and lower levels of Internet skills.

Online content use can also be supported by developers' careful anticipations. For example, in the search for information, users can be supported by limiting the number of large-scale portals. These portals often seem to achieve a result that is opposite to the intended result. Other possibilities include supporting the query-formulation process, improving text readability, providing short and focused content, and applying quality hallmarks that can only be awarded if the content is proven valid and of high quality. From a communication skill perspective, content improvement can be achieved by supporting and encouraging people in managing their online contacts, employing discussion board moderators, ensuring that people create profiles in a responsible manner, and supporting collective intelligence systems. From a content creation skill perspective, such improvement might be accomplished by providing tools that not only limit the technical knowledge needed, but also attempt to make users more aware of what they are creating. Finally, from a strategic skill perspective, content improvement can be achieved by providing decision-making support systems. These might help Internet users maintain a strong focus, take the appropriate actions, and make the correct choices. These systems can be developed for various daily life decisions that people face.

Educational solutions are the first to draw attention when people discuss the problem of a lack of digital skills. However, this is not the first thought of people who have problems in learning to use the digital media. The natural reaction is to attempt to solve the problem and learn by doing or by trial and error. Along the way, people tend to ask others in the social environment for help. We have emphasized that these are the most natural ways to learn digital skills and that they will remain the most important ways. With the improvement in technical design creating increasingly intuitive digital media, these ways will become even more important.

However, we have also stressed that these natural solutions are inadequate. This type of learning is opportunistic and misses many of the wonderful opportunities that the digital media offer. In this way, digital media are underused. Moreover, as the tasks of work, school, and leisure time are becoming overly complex, this type of learning is no longer adequate. Proximate individuals who are assumed to have answers to questions might provide the wrong answers. Finally, we have argued that these ways of learning might be a partial solution to relatively simple medium-related digital skills but not to content-related skills. Content-related skills require background knowledge, experience, practical know-how, and creativity. In many cases, they call for systematic education.

In chapter 6, we have explained that digital skills must be implemented in the curriculum of formal education at all levels. In some cases, such training must be performed in special training and classes. However, for the most part, digital skills, primarily content-related skills, can be better integrated in existing parts of the curriculum such as languages, history, geography, biology, physics, mathematics, and media education.

For people older than 40, who have not learned digital skills at school or at work, a particular type of adult education must be offered. They can visit public access sites or libraries with staff members who can teach these skills in short basic courses or answer questions and help them with a specific Internet activity. In developing countries, these are the most common places to learn digital skills for people of all ages.

Some groups in society require special treatment as a target group. These groups are the elderly, functionally illiterate individuals, the differently abled, homeless people, and migrants who do not speak the local language or English. Digital skills training should be adapted to the special needs and handicaps of these groups. This is also an important general principle for every type of digital skills education. Education should be adjusted to the needs, motivations, and local cultures of learners.

The following paragraphs discuss educational solutions in the context of current policies to solve digital skills problems.

Policy Perspectives

The discussion of contemporary policies to prevent or cure the problem of inadequate digital skills begins with a number of general principles that guide policy makers to make concrete choices among the available strategies and instruments. Subsequently, the societal actors with a responsibility in solving this problem are listed. These actors extend beyond governments and educational institutions. ICT producers, ICT training institutes, publishers of digital-learning tools, labor organizations, public access sites, libraries, user support groups, and digital media users also have tasks and responsibilities. Finally, we discuss the currently available strategies and instruments for all of these actors.

General Perspectives

All responsible actors must consider, accept, or reject a number of general insights that have arisen in this book. The first and most important is a *social-contextual perspective*, which we consider more helpful in understanding and solving the problems of inadequacies of skills than a technical perspective. Learning digital skills is not a temporary task of learning a number of tricks on a device or a series of steps in a program. When the digital media were first offered in the 1980s and 1990s, a popular view was that they required the learning of tricks on a keyboard and steps in office programs such as word processing and making spreadsheets. The tasks were considered to be temporary and primarily technical. Once people had learned these tricks and steps, they were expected to be included in the digital world.

In this book, we have argued that the social context of digital media use is much more important than the technological background. From the initial motivation to begin using digital media through reaching the benefits of this use, social and contextual factors are decisive. When people are not motivated to use particular digital media, they will not learn the skills. They will also not learn skills if they do not reach benefits because they will stop using the media. When the digital media do not fit into their everyday lives, they will only use them when strictly needed. As they have problems operating these media, they will first seek help from proximate others who are like them or have the same social background rather than visiting a remote technical helpdesk. When a particular place to learn digital skills such as a school of adult education, a public access site, or a library is not attractive, potential learners will not use these venues. If computer and Internet courses are not adapted to the learners' needs and culture, learners will learn less than expected. When features that are learned in schools or computer classes are not practiced in one's place of work, study, and leisure time, they will soon be forgotten. Throughout this book, we have frequently identified these social and contextual effects.

As a technical perspective on learning digital skills is not helpful, the *strategy of hardware provision* to potential learners is not a feasible solution. Yet, this strategy has been dominant since the start of new media development 25 years ago. The main policy in education worldwide has been to equip schools with a particular number of computers and Internet connections (Selwyn, 2013). Adapting school programs and educational software and retraining teachers were implemented much later. Public access sites and libraries were equipped with as many PCs, terminals, and printers as the budget allowed, and staff training was given a lower priority.

Equipment, software, connections, and subscriptions are necessary for learning digital skills, as is well-known worldwide. However, it would be quite enlightening to study the history of developed countries that currently have a high access rate. Government and business hardware provision programs that provide citizens and employees with tax reductions and price discounts for PCs at home have not largely contributed to physical access rates, let alone to digital skills improvement (Van Dijk, 2005). The fast adoption of "always on" home broadband access that is fully paid by the residents and provides ample opportunities for learning by doing in multimedia environments has had a greater impact on access and skills improvements than all subsidized provisions. This is not to say that developing countries can simply imitate this diffusion pattern. In these countries, collective and relatively cheap public access provision will remain the most important option for a long time to come.

In the developing countries, hardware provisions for school-going children have attracted much attention in the last 15 years. The One Laptop per Child Project and the Indian Hole in the Wall Project have become famous for their idealist effort. Below, these projects will be critically discussed as clear examples of an overly technical orientation on digital skills learning that neglects the social, cultural, and educational environment.

A technical and hardware orientation is also responsible for a perspective on digital skills that completely focuses on operational and formal skills, that is, skills related to the technical medium. This perspective has completely dominated digital skills learning programs in the last 25 years. In this book, we have argued for a perspective that *combines technical and substantive views*, drawing much attention to content-related digital skills. Isolated computer courses and trainings that only teach medium-related skills and pay little or no attention to the substantial knowledge, experience, and know-how needed in digital media use will only have a small and temporary effect. They might help people who otherwise would not achieve access to the digital world and can find their own way as soon as they have crossed the operational threshold, but the skills learned in this manner will soon be outdated as technology moves forward and practical applications of the digital media require more substantial knowledge and other (practical) skills.

A fourth appropriate general policy perspective is to adopt a clear *target group strategy* in the education and improvement of digital skills. The first impulse of most educational institutions and computer course organizers is to standardize and certify digital skills in a number of operations and instructions for all to follow for particular applications, primarily office programs, email, and general Internet use. It is doubtful whether standardization and certification lead to effective learning strategies. They clarify and specify the goals of learning but are not sufficiently adapted to the special needs of user groups. In chapter 6, we discussed the special treatments that the elderly, the differently abled, illiterate individuals, and migrants must receive in learning digital skills. Such a target group approach might also be helpful for categories of learners who are not disadvantaged in a special way. For example, on-the-job training of digital skills and skills courses that are adapted to workers' tasks might be more effective than standard courses.

A target group approach comes close to the perspective of adapting all solutions to the digital skills problem (both design and educational solutions) to *individual needs and local cultures*. The design of digital media can be made more attractive for user groups when it is customized to their needs (for example, all options of a particular device or program are offered while only a fraction is needed) or local culture (e.g., one's own language). Courses and training can be built around contents and assignments that are appealing to the learners concerned. Adaption to individual and local needs serves the main driver of digital skills acquisition: motivation.

Policy Actors Engaged

Solving the problem of inadequate digital skills, the main theme of the second part of this book, is the task of many actors and institutions in society. It cannot be completed by, for example, schools, libraries, and public access centers only. The policy to solve this problem is the responsibility of many actors in society, including governments, ICT industry, ICT training, software and content publishers, labor organizations, schools and universities, libraries, public access centers, and user support groups. Only governments are able to attempt to coordinate this diversity of actors. Thus, we begin the discussion with governments as policy actors.

Governments

Both national and local governments feel a responsibility to help solve the problem of a lack of digital skills among people in their constituency. The motivation to do this is derived from their economic, innovation, educational, social, and cultural policies. Economic policy is driven by the observation that adequate digital skills lead to more business opportunities for national and local corporations and better employment opportunities for individual job-seekers. Innovation policy is partially built on the assumption that a population that is sufficiently skilled in one of the main contemporary sectors of innovation is a solid base for future innovation in this sector, the sector of information and communication technology. This is a prime reason for the European Union, for example, to invest billions of euros in the research and development of instruments to improve digital skills. Educational policy requires a continual update of facilities, curricula, and teacher qualifications in schools. Finally, social and cultural policy related to ICT diffusion is needed to enable citizens to live in an information society and to utilize, among others, electronic public services.

Governments have a wide range of instruments at their disposal to support digital skills improvement. These instruments are listed in box 7.1. The first action that governments consider is to provide the *necessary infrastructure*, first, in schools. They consider that without access to the latest technology, citizens and students at all levels of education are not able to use the technology and develop skills. For example, one of the reasons that the US government currently prioritizes broadband diffusion in America is that broadband enables many more types of applications for citizens, students, workers, and businesses that motivate them to develop skills. However, in most countries, the most important action is to provide all schools with as many computer terminals and Internet connections as the budget allows.

Once governments discover that hardware provision does not solve every digital skill problem, they charge researchers with the job of *framework building*: What exactly is needed for digital skills? The first job is to develop operational definitions of all skills concerned, as has been done in this book. The second job is to standardize and certify these skills and to transform them into new curricula.

The third instrument is to *raise awareness* among the population and the leadership of local institutions that inadequate digital skills are an important problem that is not automatically solved by infrastructure provision only. After the year 2000, responsible governments became aware of this and installed research and policy groups to investigate this problem and to inform businesses, schools, and other public institutions that this problem required special attention. In some cases, this was accompanied by concrete policy proposals.

Closely linked to raising awareness, government initiatives *organize stakeholders* in this field and encourage them to work together to propose a national or local policy to solve the problem. Stakeholder organization varies in scope: it can be quite broad, engaging organizations of employers, employees, local businesses, formal educational institutions, organizations for adult education, public libraries, and municipalities, and it can also be more limited, uniting companies that require computer training with computer course services in private and public-private partnerships. The broad initiatives are typically initiated by governments, whereas small-scale initiatives are private actions.

A fifth government instrument is *educational policy* at every level. In most countries, governments are responsible for public education and the continual renovation this requires. The advent of digital media such as computers and Internet applications in school classes has stimulated permanent renewal of school curricula, teacher training, educational software, and didactical innovation. Ministries of Education investigate, propose, and pay for such improvements.

Governments have an interest in stimulating their citizens to use *government information and transaction services*. Some governments seize the opportunity to support citizens in using these services and learning digital skills in this way. Some countries offer special courses to learn to use digital service desks. In other cases, civil servants help citizens in using eservices when they arrive at personal service desks.

The final government instrument is *public access provision* in public libraries, community centers, and other public buildings. A link to digital skills is added when available staff has sufficient expertise and time to support the users in these public places or when special computer and Internet courses are provided.

Box 7.1 Government Instruments to Support Digital Skills

- Infrastructure provision;
- Framework building and standardization of digital skills;
- Raising awareness in society;
- Stakeholder organization; partnership building;
- Educational policies;
- Public eservices training;
- Public access provision and support.

ICT Industry

The ICT industry has initiated the digital skills problem by supplying technology that is relatively difficult to use. This actor is also able to alleviate a large part of this problem by producing more user-friendly hardware and software. In chapter 5, we also suggested several ways that developers and designers can account for lower levels of content-related skills. The recent turn to intuitive and easy-to-operate devices such as smartphones and tablets has reduced medium-related digital skill problems. However, it has done little to diminish content-related skills problems. In fact, we suggested that the move toward mobile devices will lead to an increase in the so-called usage gap because the freedom to perform content-related skills in mobile services and having a user-generated creative input is much more controlled and limited by the application than in desktops and laptops with complete functionality. Thus, the shift toward mobile devices might even accelerate the usage gaps between people who use desktop computers and laptops with advanced functions and people who rely on mobile devices with limited and largely preprogrammed functions.

ICT Training Institutes

General computer and Internet training institutes, for example, those that issue so-called computer driver's licenses, are able to define the standards and certificates of every module of computer and Internet skills required. Specific training institutes that focus on particular professionals such as health professionals or bank employees do the same for more specialized skills. In these cases, the share of content-related skills is higher than that in general institutes that typically focus on the command of office programs. Both types of training institutes largely define digital skills according to public opinion. Typically, this is a rather technical or instrumental view of skills. These institutes have a long way ahead to standardize and certify the content-related skills that are discussed in this book. Most likely, general institutes will not perform these tasks because they consider them to be the job of the professional institutes that specialize in profession-related content. These professional institutes are relatively new. The general institutes have a record of providing many thousands of courses every year in most countries of the world.

Publishers of Learning Tools

Good educational software for training digital skills is rare. Therefore, publishers of learning tools such as self-assessments of people's skills, computer books, and DVDs or CDs containing good audiovisual instruction and assignments for all six skills described in this book have an important job. These tools have an advanced portion for teachers and a portion for the pupils, students, workers, or job-seekers as end users.

These publishers have two main problems. First, their tools are quickly outdated due to rapid changes in hardware and software. Second, their market is relatively small because many people believe that they can better learn on the job or by trial and error under good personal guidance. The market for teachers' books is also fairly small. Other students prefer to use the books or help functions that are published with every new version of a popular office application. These books are piling up in book shops.

Labor Organizations

One of the main conclusions of the 2011 nationwide survey of the Dutch labor force discussed in the former chapter was that in this country—and we expect many others—company management leaves employees on their own in solving digital skill-related problems. Management typically does not realize how many productive hours are lost by malfunctioning ICT and the inadequate skills of their employees. Less than one-quarter of these employees responded that they learned the most from formal training and helpdesks, regular solutions offered by management. However, employees attempted various types of informal solutions for skills problems such as learning by doing and asking colleagues and people outside of work. Respondents underestimated the return on investment of formal schooling and training of digital skills (Van Deursen & Van Dijk, 2014b).

Thus, raising awareness of the problem and its potential solutions among the management of labor organizations seems to be the first priority here. A large number of effective measures could then be taken. A first option is to institutionalize the currently informal assistance of colleagues. Employees with excellent digital skills and some didactic competencies could be appointed the special task of assistance. A collective of these helpers from all departments could create a network that collaborates with the helpdesk (when available). Some organizations have provided new employees with a so-called *ICT buddy* for various questions related to digital media use.

A second solution might be to reevaluate the role of helpdesks in organizations. Typically, the image of helpdesks is rather technical, only assisting when technical accidents occur. Most helpdesk assistants are not models of didactic expertise. Nevertheless, helpdesks could be charged with the broader task of assisting in training and explanations to prevent the failures in commanding hardware and software that often occur. For this shift in task perception, they should be trained in didactic skills.

Another need is to shift the priorities of digital skills training from providing courses in traditional computer business applications and office programs to skills needed for Internet and smartphone applications used at work. These relatively new skills are strongly neglected in labor organizations. Management, white-collar workers, and office personnel require these skills. An inventory can be made of smartphone and Internet applications that have the most useful purposes for the tasks of the workplace concerned.

An important management job is to screen the digital skill levels of all categories of workers by means of more or less extensive self-assessments or performance tests, with particular attention to the needs of seniors and the less educated. Young workers should also be screened, as organizations should not expect to automatically secure digital skills by hiring new young employees.

The result of this screening might be an inventory of the need for courses or training on the job or in computer classes offered by external educational institutions. The current research indicates that courses and training are more effective than the trainees anticipated.

Finally, special attention should be paid to email skills. They are an important source of productivity loss because email is used much longer and less efficiently than necessary, as explained in chapters 2 and 4.

Schools and Universities

Schools have the advantage that they are the first institutions that governments and other financiers such as charity organizations consider to support ICT and digital skills in education. By far, the greatest priority has been given to technology provision, that is, equipping schools with hardware and software. Plans to support digital skills development are not given priority. These plans typically list teacher training as the top priority; however, such training often comes last or does not occur at all.

In primary education, most attention is given to teaching children operational and formal skills above the skills that they developed in preschool and at home. In modern schools, computers are used to learn to read, write, and calculate. In secondary education, attention shifts to content-related digital skills, that is, primarily information skills (at least, that is the hope). Some teachers give students take-home assignments or other homework and allow them to use the Internet to complete the assignments. Unfortunately, many of these teachers do not give adequate instruction in, for instance, the use of search engines and the composition of papers largely derived from Internet sources. Many teachers tend to forget that their students' information, communication, and strategic skills are insufficient and that they have a large role in teaching them. This is even true for colleges and universities, as students are expected to enter with the information skills and other content-related skills required. The current performance tests among the higher educated show that this assumption is inaccurate in many cases (see chapter 4).

The main didactic principle should be to benefit from a mutual inspiration of ways or styles that children and students have developed in their home environment and the learning methods that are used at school, employing both traditional and digital media. Currently, these styles are often worlds apart. When pupils or students are allowed to employ their own methods of digital media use, they become motivated. They tend to listen to the suggestions that teachers provide to improve their content-related skills in particular school subjects.

In the former chapter, we have suggested that it is preferable to embed the learning of content-related digital skills in existing school subjects than in new or special subjects. This is especially true for information, and strategic skills that can be embedded in language courses, history, geography, biology, physics, and mathematics. Communication skills, content creation skills and the strategic skills required in media use could be addressed in relatively new subjects such as media education or information science.

To realize this innovation, educational institutions typically begin with curriculum development. Specific goals of learning, required competencies, and guidelines for computer and Internet education must be devised. Additionally, many teachers must be retrained and given the time to create new didactic contents for a digital media environment.

Public Libraries

In all countries, both developed and developing, public libraries have a generally accepted function of supplying access, offering assistance, and providing computer and Internet classes. However, the scope and scale of the activities differ based on the task perception of public libraries. Do they prioritize the tasks of access, assistance, and education with respect to the digital media? In the United States, for example, the priority is rated very high, whereas public libraries in some other countries have a fairly traditional perception of their role and focus on print media. In some countries, public libraries take a very active and stimulating role. In other countries, libraries may be more reactive and wait for visitors to request assistance. In addition to the statistics reported in the former chapter, in 2011, the highest percentage of US public libraries (nearly 80 percent) offered point-of-use assistance, followed by formal training classes (38 percent), one-on-one trainings (28 percent), and online training material (29 percent). See Bertot, McDermott, Lincoln, Real, and Peterson (2011) and Jaeger, Bertot, Thompson, Katz, and Decoster (2012) for more detailed statistics.

Visitors to public libraries may have different needs. Some guests have a high level of skills and visit the library to have more or less free wireless access. Others have no access at home and a very low level of skills; they primarily seek computer and Internet access. Other guests request assistance with a particular task that requires information or strategic skills. This is the core expertise of libraries. Public libraries and their staff take a rather different attitude to potential requests for assistance. Some staff members wait for visitors to come to a service desk, whereas others walk around, observe, and ask whether help is needed. Invitations to follow particular computer and Internet courses depend on the program, the expertise, and the number of staff members that can be offered. For this intensive and expensive task, many public libraries lack the necessary funding or budgets.

Public and Community Access Centers

The tasks and opportunities of public and community access sites are similar to those of public libraries. Their tasks are to offer access to people without a computer or Internet connection at home or at work or who need a wireless hot spot, guidance in using these media when they have particular questions, and longer lasting courses in digital skills. The main difference is that access centers have a larger social function than the average public library. This function is related to the public function concerned (e.g., health service in a hospital, public services in a government building, and adult education in a public school). Community centers have a social and cultural function for proximate neighborhoods, as they aid in organizing communities. New Internet applications and online communities can be a motive for particular community initiatives. These facilities might stimulate the rise of online communities.

The function of public and community access centers in regard to digital access and skills greatly differs in low- and high-access countries, or in developing and developed nations. In low-access countries and developing nations, they have a crucial and indispensable role in providing access to the majority of people with scarce resources and skills. They also play an important role as meeting places, particularly for young people. In the former chapter, we have demonstrated that even commercial Internet cafés may serve these functions.

In high-access countries and developed nations, the functions of public and community access centers are much more focused on specific tasks. As home access is widely available in these countries, they offer wireless access and fixed access to the small portion of the population without home access. They are not general meeting places for the entire population, but for particular groups that are engaged in health support, community building, immigration courses, political association, or so on. Computer or Internet training targets particular groups, such as the elderly, immigrants, differently abled people, or patient groups.

In both types of countries, public and community access centers must be embedded in the local culture and adapted to the specific needs of the people who visit them. These centers comprise collective activities that differ from the individual approach that dominates the activities of public libraries and computer or Internet adult education institutions. These collective activities, such as community action, have goals and functions that might not be related to individual digital skills training.

User Support Services and Citizen Initiatives

The responsibility for the improvement of digital skills extends beyond public institutions and companies. Individual users, consumers, and citizens also have a responsibility to improve their digital skills. First, they must make a realistic estimation of their skills. Second, they must seek solutions in terms of social support or education. The Internet offers many applications for these needs. Self-assessment tests of digital skills are available in several countries. In all countries, people can search for courses and trainings both online and offline. For most people who are sufficiently motivated to learn digital skills, there is a solution, even in poor countries. For example, they could spend time in an Internet café, talk to people and become informed, or consult a friend or acquaintance with digital experience.

In addition to individual initiatives, there are many collective initiatives of citizens, consumers, and users in general. In all countries, several senior-webs have been organized. They offer information, assistance, and courses that are adapted to the special needs of the elderly. The same is true for differently abled individuals, immigrants, and low-literacy groups. These initiatives have a commercial basis and rely on public subsidies. The authors of this book believe that the individual and collective activities discussed here should have much stronger social, public, and government support. With small additional means, these activities could be extremely effective.

A List of Strategies and Instruments for Digital Skills Improvement

At the end of this book, we provide a synopsis of the main practical strategies and instruments to solve the digital skills problem. It is condensed because we do not intend to present a fully developed action plan. The strategies and instrument are clustered and listed in box 7.2.

Box 7.2   Clusters of Strategies and Instruments for Digital Skills Improvement

AWARESS AND ORGANIZATION
- Awareness programs
- Stakeholder organization
- Public-private partnerships
- Monitoring current skills
- Self-assessments

DESIGN IMPROVEMENT
- Increase accessibility and usability
- Adapt hardware and software for the differently abled, seniors, low literates, and migrants

TECHNOLOGY PROVISION
- Infrastructure provision
- One Laptop per Child type of projects
- Public access provision
- Special tools for the disabled and others

CONTENT DEVELOPMENT
- Framework building (what skills?)
- Standardization, certification, and curriculum development
- Educational software
- Content target groups

EDUCATION
- Specific curriculum change
- Teacher training
- Institutionalized courses and training
- On the job training and personal guidance in other contexts

Awareness and Organization

Large sections of society are not yet aware of the seriousness and impact of the inequality of digital skills problem, which inspired the writing of this book. When governments, corporations, school authorities, and institutions of adult education discover the scope and scale of this problem, they might organize awareness programs. These programs should call attention to the problem and provide concrete solutions that make sense to the people concerned.

Often, multiple actors might be involved in this problem and its solutions. The institutions with the largest scope, such as national or local governments and educational institutions, should take the initiative to join all relevant stakeholders. Responsible government departments, most interested businesses, schools, and computer course institutions are common combinations. This collective enterprise often entails public-private partnerships that work with a combination of material and immaterial (skills improvement) profits and the public interest.

It is the job of government departments such Ministries of Education, the economy, and innovation to monitor the current level of skills of the population, both workers and citizens. In this respect, the authors of this book monitor the skills of the Dutch general and labor population in annual trend surveys of Internet use charged by the Dutch ministry of Economy and Innovation. This is accomplished by proxy survey questions that help to estimate the current level of the six skills discussed in this book. Monitoring requires the choice of a particular framework with operational definitions of digital skills.

Monitoring can also be performed through the completion of self-assessments of skills on the Internet. An online self-assessment based on the current framework can be found at www.internetbootcamp.nl. Online self-assessments should also contain suggestions to address specific inadequate skills.

Design Improvement

In chapter 5, we have discussed many ways to improve the accessibility and usability of hardware and software to prevent digital skills problems. We suggested particular ways to improve interfaces and online content that would benefit many people, not only those with disabilities. Many people seem to struggle with Internet use because the implemented designs are overly difficult to use. This is worrisome because information and services are often offered online with the expectation that all individuals able to use them. Over the last few years, similar trends have been observed for applications that are specifically designed for mobile computers.

Technology Provision

Adequate infrastructure is a necessary condition for learning digital skills. This should be a particular focus of attention in developing nations. However, a strong emphasis on infrastructure provision can also be called easy thinking. The results in terms of skills and usage might be quite disappointing when insufficient attention is paid to the implementation and user support of ICTs. Equipping schools with hardware, software, and Internet connections is the first action that governments and educational institutions consider in terms of educational innovation in the field of ICTs. All other measures are a second thought.

Examples of this technical orientation include a number of technology provision projects in the Third World that specifically address children. In the Hole in the Wall project in India, kiosks were installed in streets to provide children with access to a limited number of computer and Internet applications but with little guidance or skill support. In the famous 2005 One Laptop per Child Project (OLCP) in several developing countries, a selection of children have been provided with a cheap ($200 or less) but sturdy laptop.

Both these examples of technology provision ignore the social, cultural, educational, and material context in which they operate. Warschauer and Ames (2010) and Selwyn (2013) wage sharp criticism against the OLCP's "technocentric vision," "the latest in a long line of technologically Utopian development schemes that have unsuccessfully attempted to solve complex social problems with overly simplistic solutions"(Warschauer & Ames, 2010, p. 33). Warschauer and Ames provide a detailed description of these projects, focusing on the affordability of a laptop program for the targeted countries (high- and middle-income developing countries, not the poorest), the flawed expectations about the effects of implementation without much guidance in educational environments, problems with the design of the special operating system and broken hardware parts, and the disappointing realities of student use only benefitting the children with the best school performance. "Instead of a approach of simply handing computers to children and walking away, there needs to be large-scale integrated education improvement efforts" (p. 34). They argue that "the poorest countries targeted by OLPC cannot afford laptop computers for all their children and would be better off building schools, training teachers, developing curricula, providing books and subsidizing attendance"(p. 34).

Public access provision and special hardware tools for the disabled and the elderly have more immediate positive results of technology provision. They do not offer complete solutions but provide a last push to people who are motivated—otherwise they would not visit these sites or request these tools—and they are typically accompanied by support of a more or less professional staff.

Content Development

The most substantial task in solving the digital-divide problem is to investigate which digital skills are needed and to build a conceptual framework of the result. One such framework has been developed in this book. The current framework of six types of skills focuses on the Internet skills every user requires to command this medium in a satisfactory manner. However, in the context of jobs, occupations, or professions, at a particular school level or in particular public or private services, more specific frameworks are often needed. Every job requires a particular set of skills. University students require more advanced skills than students of secondary education. The use of eGovernment services such as electronic tax file completion requires skills that differ from those needed on eCommerce sites.

Once a particular framework is developed, professional organizations in particular areas and course institutions that offer computer and Internet trainings must make the framework operational by means of standardization, certification, and curriculum development. Modules of particular skills are composed. These modules conclude with tests or exams and certification in diplomas or testimonials. For every module, a curriculum and courseware are developed. An important conclusion of this book is that current modules are overly focused on medium-related skills and that the content-related information, communication, content creation and strategic skills are strongly neglected or even absent. For these skills, much operational work remains to be performed. Many modules can be added to the typical modules of office software in general Internet use.

The following step, the development of educational software and courseware that are appropriate for specific contexts and target groups of users, is the most crucial step. The quality of educational software and courseware is decisive for every computer course or training. This book has argued that these trainings should be adapted to the social, cultural, and practical needs of the target groups concerned.

Education

When the frameworks, standards, and certificates of digital skills courses or trainings are prepared and educational institutions are ready to use them, these institutions must adapt their curricula and prepare their teachers for elearning. This typically involves teacher training. The focus and content of the required training should be known. The type of curriculum change determines whether the focus should be medium-related or content-related digital skills. In the former chapter, we strongly suggested that most learning of digital skills, particularly the content-related skills, should be integrated in existing school subjects. The last section of this chapter specified these school subjects. The integration of content-related skills in existing topics clearly motivates teachers more than the separation in special classes. In this way, teachers will discover that their expertise adds to digital skills in a narrower sense, most often the medium-related skills over which they believe their students have greater command.

The second most important context for education, learning digital skills for work, has a choice between on-the-job training and separate or remote computer and Internet classes offered by schools or training institutes of adult and computer education. For the most part, on-the-job training is the most effective and efficient method. However, for concentrated effort in learning without job distractions, outside classes and training might be preferred.

The difference between on-the-job training and outside learning shows that learning digital skills should not be viewed as a narrow instrumental task. In this book, we have attempted to show that learning digital skills is a social-contextual affair that is completely embedded in social and everyday relationships. We have also argued that education is not the only solution for a lack of digital skills. Preventive measures of improving technical design are equally as important. Finally, we have attempted to clarify that policy choices regarding social and information inequality in general, such as job creation and school investment, might provide the most effective contribution in the long-term to the improvement of digital skills as the key to the information society.

References

Alexander, J. E., & Tate, M. A. (1999). *Web wisdom: How to evaluate and create information quality on the Web*. Hillsdale, NJ: Erlbaum.

Alfieri, L., Brooks, P. J., Aldrich, N. J., & Tenenbaum, H. R. (2011). Does discovery-based instruction enhance learning? *Journal of Educational Psychology, 103*(1) (February), 1–18.

Anttiroiko, A.V., Lintilä, L., & Savolainen, R. (2001). Information society competencies of managers: Conceptual considerations. In E. Pantzar, R. Savolainen, & P. Tynjälä (Eds.), *In search for a human-centered information society* (pp. 27–57). Tampere: Tampere University Press.

Attewell, P. (2001). The first and second digital divides. *Sociology of Education, 74*(3), 252–259.

Aula, A., & Nordhausen, K. (2006). Modeling successful performance in Web searching. *Journal of the American Society for Information Science and Technology, 57*(12), 1678–1693.

Ba, H., Tally, W., & Tsikalas, K. (2002). Investigating children's emerging digital literacies. *The Journal of Technology, Learning, and Assessment, 1*(4), 1–49.

Bawden, D. (2001). Information and digital literacies: A review of concepts. *Journal of Documentation, 57*(2), 218–259.

Bawden, D. (2008). Origins and concepts of digital literacy. In C. Lankshear & M. Knobel (Eds.), *Digital literacy: Concepts, policies and practices* (pp. 17–32). New York: Peter Lang.

Bean, C. (2003). Meeting the Challenge: Training an aging population to use computers. *The Southeastern Librarian, 51*(3), article 6.

Bean, L., & Hott, D. D. (2005). Wiki: A speedy new tool to manage projects. *Journal of Corporate Accounting & Finance, 16*(5), 3–8.

Becker, S., Crandall, M. D., Fisher, K. E., Blakewood, R., Kinney, B., & Russell-Sauvé, C. (2011). *Opportunity for all: How library policies and practices impact public Internet access*. Washington, DC: Institute of Museum and Library Services.

Beitzel, S. M., Jensen, E. C., Chowdhury, A., Grossman, D., & Frieder, O. (2004). Hourly analysis of a very large topically categorized Web query log. In P. D. Bruza & J. Thom (Eds.), *Proceedings of the 27th annual international conference on research and development in information retrieval* (pp. 321–328). Sheffield, UK: SIGIS.

Beniger, J. R. (1986). *The control revolution: Technological and economic origins of the information society.* Cambridge, MA: Harvard University Press.

Benigeri, M., & Pluye, P. (2003). Shortcomings of health information on the Internet. *Health Promotion International, 18*(4), 381–386.

Bennett, S., Maton, K., & Kevin, L. (2008). The "digital natives" debate: A critical review of the evidence. *British Journal of Educational Technology, 39*(5), 775–786.

Berners-Lee, T., & Fischetti, M. (2000). *Weaving the web: The original design and ultimate destiny of the World Wide Web.* New York, NY: Harpercollins.

Bertot, J. (2010). Community-based e-government: Libraries as e-government partners and providers. *Lecture Notes in Computer Science 6228*, 121–131.

Bertot, J., McDermott, A., Lincoln, R., Real, B., & Peterson, K. (2011). Public library funding and technology access survey: Survey findings and results. Information Policy and Access Center, University of Maryland College Park.

Bilal, D. (2000). Children's use of the Yahooligans! Web search engine: I. Cognitive, physical, and affective behaviors on fact-based search tasks. *Journal of the American Society of Information Science, 51*, 646–665.

Bimber, B. (2003). *Information and American democracy.* New York, NY: Cambridge University Press.

Birru, M. S., Monaco, V. M., Charles, L., Drew, H., Njie, V., Bierria, T., . . . Steinman, R. A. (2004). Internet usage by low-literacy adults seeking health information: An observational analysis. *Journal of Medical Internet Research, 6*(3), e25.

Bishop, A. P., Neumann, L. J., Star, S. L., Merkel, C., Ignacio, E. & Sandusky, R. J. (2000). Digital libraries: Situating use in changing information infrastructure. *Journal of the American Society for Information Science, 51*, 394–413.

Boechler, P. M. (2001). How spatial is hyperspace? Interacting with hypertext documents: Cognitive processes and concepts. *CyberPsychology and Behavior, 4*, 23–46.

Bonfadelli, H. (2002). The Internet and knowledge gaps: A theoretical and empirical investigation. *European Journal of Communication, 17*(1), 65–84.

Boyd, D. (2006). Friends, friendsters, and mySpace top 8: Writing community into being on social network sites. *First Monday, 11*(12). Retrieved March 14, 2007, from http://www.firstmonday.org/issues/issue11_12/boyd/.

Boyd, D. (2007). Error: You must be someone's friend to comment on them. Paper presented at the annual conference of International Communication Association, San Francisco.

Boyd, D., & Bee, H. (2009). *Lifespan Development.* Boston: Pearson.

Brake, D. R. (2014). Are we all online content creators now? Web 2.0 and digital divides. *Journal of Computer-Mediated Communication, 19*(3), 591–609.

Brand-Gruwel, S., Wopereis, I., & Vermetten, Y. (2005). Information problem solving by experts and novices: Analysis of a complex cognitive skill. *Computers in Human Behavior, 21*(3), 487–508.

Bridge IT Thematic Network. (2010). *Guidelines on ICT solutions for social inclusion and cultural diversity*. Retrieved July 27, 2012, from http://www.bridge-it-net.eu/.

Britt, A. M., & Aglinskas, C. (2002). Improving students' ability to identify and use source information. *Cognition and Instruction, 20*, 485–522.

Brundidge, J., & Rice, R. E. (2009). Political engagement and exposure to heterogeneous political discussion: Do the (information) rich get richer and the similar get more similar? In A. Chadwick & P. N. Howard (Eds.), *The handbook of Internet politics*. London: Routledge.

Bruner, J. S. (1961). The act of discovery. *Harvard Educational Review, 31*(1), 21–32.

Bruner, J. S., & Olson, D. R. (1973). Learning through experience and learning through media. In G. Gerbner, L. Gross, & W. Melody (Eds.), *Communications, technology and social policy*. New York: Wiley.

Buckingham, D. (2012). *Beyond technology: Children's learning in the age of digital culture*. Cambridge: Polity.

Buente, W., & Robbin, A. (2008). Trends in Internet information behavior, 2000–2004. *Journal of the American Society for Information Science and Technology, 59*(1), 1743–1760.

Bullen, M., Morgan, T., & Qayyum, A. (2011). Digital learners in higher education: Generation is not the issue. *Canadian Journal of Learning and Technology, 37*(1), 1–18.

Bunz, U. (2004). The computer-email-web (CEW) fluency scale—Development and validation. *International Journal of Human-Computer Interaction, 17*(4), 479–506.

Bunz, U. (2009). A generational comparison of gender, computer anxiety, and computer-email-web fluency. *Studies in Media & Information Literacy Education, 9*(2), 54–69.

Castells, M. (1998). *End of millennium, the information age: Economy, society and culture*. Oxford, UK: Blackwell.

Castells, M. (2002). *The Internet galaxy: Reflections of the Internet, business, and society*. Oxford: Oxford University Press.

Carvin, A. (2000). *More than just access: Fitting literacy and content into the digital divide equation*. http://net.educause.edu/ir/library/pdf/ERM0063.pdf.

Chen, J., Geyer, W., Dugan, C., Muller, M., & Guy, I. (2009). Make new friends, but keep the old—recommending people on social networking sites. *CHI 2009 Online Relationships*, April 6, Boston, MA, USA.

Chen, S.Y., & Macredie, R. D. (2002). Cognitive style and hypermedia navigation: Development of a learning model. *Journal of the American Society for Information Science and Technology, 53*, 3–15.

Ciolek, T. M. (1996). Today's WWW, tomorrow's MMM: The specter of multimedia mediocrity. *IEEE COMPUTER, 29*(1), 106–108.

Coiro, J., & Dobler, E. (2007). Exploring the online reading comprehension strategies used by sixth-grade skilled readers to search for and locate information on the Internet. *Reading Research Quarterly, 42*, 214–257.

Correa, T., Willard Hinsley, A., & Gil de Zuniga, H. (2010).Who interacts on the web? The intersection of users' personality and social media use. *Computers in Human Behavior, 26*(2), 247–253.

Correa, T., Straubhaar, J. D., Spence, J., & Chen, W. (2012). Brokering new technologies: The role of children in their parents' usage of the Internet. Paper presented at the 62nd Annual Conference of the International Communication Association, Phoenix, Arizona, May 24–28.

Cox, M., Webb, M., Abbott, C., Blakeley, B., Beauchamp, T., & Rhodes, V. (2004). *A review of the research literature relating to ICT and attainment.* London: Becta.

Czaja, S. (1997). Computer technology and the older adult. In M. G. Helander, T. K. Landauer, P.V. Prabhu (Eds.), *Handbook of human-computer interaction.* New York: Elsevier.

D'Alessandro, D. M., Kingsley, P., & Johnson-West, J. (2001). The readability of pediatric patient education materials on the World Wide Web. *Archives of Pediatrics and Adolescent Medicine, 155*(7), 807–812.

Danielson, D. R. (2003). Transitional volatility in web navigation: Usability metrics and user behavior. *IT&Society, 1*(3), 131–158.

Danis, C., & Singer, D. A. (2008). Wiki instance in the enterprise: Opportunities, concerns and reality. Proceedings of the 2008 {ACM} New York (NY) conference on Computer supported cooperative work, 495–504.

Davison, E. L., & Cotten, S. R. (2009). *Connection disparities: The importance of broadband connections in understanding today's digital divide.* In E. Feroo, Y. K. Dwivedi, J. R. Gil-Garcia & M. D. Williams (Eds.). Overcoming digital divides: Constructing an equitable and competitive information society. Hershey, PA: IGI Global.

Dean, R. (2009). *Taming the e-mail beast.* LaVergne, TN: Sortis Publishing.

De Castell, S., & Luke, A. (1988). Defining "literacy" in North American schools: Social and historical conditions and consequences. In E. R. Kingten, B. M. Kroll, & M. Rose (Eds.), *Perspectives on literacy* (pp. 159–174). Carbondale, IL: Southern Illinois University Press.

De Haan, J., & Huysmans, F. (2002). *Van huis uit digitaal; verwerving van digitale vaardigheden tussen thuismilieu en school.* The Hague: Sociaal en Cultureel Planbureau.

Derlega, V., Winstead, B., Wong, P., & Greenspan, M. (1987). Self-disclosure and relationship development: An attributional analysis. In M. E. Roloff & G. R. Miller (Eds.), *Interpersonal processes: New directions in communication research* (pp. 172–187). Thousand Oak, CA: Sage.

De Vries, B., Van der Meij, H., & Lazonder, A.W. (2008). Supporting reflective web searching in elementary schools. *Computers in Human Behavior, 24*, 649–665.

Devins, D., Darlow, A., & Smith, V. (2002). Lifelong learning and digital exclusion: Lessons from the evaluation of a ICT learning centre and an emerging research agenda. *Regional Studies, 36*(8), 941–945.

DiMaggio, P., & Bonikowski, B. (2008). Make money surfing the Web? The impact of Internet use on the earnings of U.S. workers. *American Sociological Review, 73*, 227–250.

DiMaggio, P., & Hargittai, E. (2001). From the "Digital divide" to "Digital inequality": Studying Internet use as penetration increases. Working Paper Series 15, Princeton, NJ: University Center for Arts and Cultural Policy Studies.

DiMaggio, P., Hargittai, E., Celeste, C., & Shafer, S. (2004). From unequal access to differentiated use: A literature review and agenda for research on digital inequality. In Neckerman, K. (Ed.), *Social Inequality* (pp. 355–400). New York, NY: Russell Sage Foundation.

Dinet, J., Favart, M., & Passerault J-M. (2004). Searching for information in an Online Public Access Catalogue (OPAC): The impacts of information search expertise on the use of Boolean operators. *Journal of Computer Assisted Learning, 20*, 336–346.

Dobransky, K., & Hargittai, E. (2006). The disability divide in Internet access and use. *Information, Communication & Society, 9*(3), 313–334.

Duijkers, H. M., Gulikers-Dinjens, M. T. H., & Boshuizen, H. P. A. (2001). Begeleiden van leerlingen bij het zoeken, selecteren en beoordelen van informatie. In J. Ahlers, T. Hoogbergen, P. Leenheer, & J. de Vos (Eds.), *Handboek Studiehuis Tweede Fase.* Alphen a/d Rijn: Samsom.

Ellison, N., Heino, R., & Gibbs, J. (2006). Managing impression online: Self-presentation processes in the online dating environment. *Journal of Computer-Mediated Communication, 11*(2), 415–441, article 2.

Ellison, N., Steinfield, C., & Lampe, C. (2007). The benefits of Facebook "friends": Exploring the relationship between college students' use of online social networks and social capital. *Journal of Computer-Mediated Communication, 12*(3), 1143–1168, article 1.

Eshet-Alkalai, Y. (2004). Digital Literacy: A conceptual framework for survival skills in the digital era. *Journal of Educational Multimedia and Hypermedia, 13*(1), 93–106.

Eurostat Statistics. (2013). Computers and the Internet in households and enterprises. Retrieved March 9, 2014, from http://epp.eurostat.ec.europa.eu.

Fidel, R., Davies, R. K., Douglass, M. H., Holder, J. K., Hopkins, C. J., Kushner, E. J.,…Toney, C. D. (1999). A visit to the information mall: Web searching behavior of high school students. *Journal of the American Society of Information Science, 50*(1), 24–37.

Fiegen, A. M., Cherry, B., & Watson, K. (2002). Reflections on collaboration: Learning outcomes and information literacy assessment in the business curriculum. *Reference Services Review, 30*(4), 307–318.

Ford, N., & Miller, D. (1996). Gender differences in Internet perceptions and use. *Aslib Proceedings, 48*(7–8), 183–192.

Gauntlett, D. (2011). *Making is connecting: The social meaning of creativity. From DIY and knitting to YouTube and Web 2.0.* London: Polity Press.

Gilster, P. (1997). *Digital literacy.* New York: Wiley.

Golder, S. A., Wilkinson, D. M., & Huberman, B. A. (2007). Rhythms of social interaction: Messaging within a massive online network. In C. Steinfield, B. Pentland, M. Ackerman, & N. Contractor (Eds.), *Proceedings of Third International Conference on Communities and Technologies* (pp. 41–66). London, UK: ACM.

Goldin, C., & Katz, L. F. (2008). *The race between education and technology*. Cambridge, MA: The Belknap Press of Harvard University.

Gong, J., & Tarasewich, P. (2004). Guidelines for handheld device interface design. *The 35th Annual Meeting of the Decision Science Institute*, November 20–23, Boston, MA, 3751–3576.

Goss, E. P., & Phillips, J. M. (2002). How information technology affects wages: Evidence using Internet usage as a proxy for IT skills. *Journal of Labor Research, 23*(3), 463–474.

Gould, J. D., & Lewis, C. (1985). Designing for usability-key principles and what designers think. Proceedings of the ACM SIGCHI San Fransico Conference on Human Factors in Computing Systems, 50–53.

Goulding, A. & Spacey, R. (2003). Women and the Information Society: Barriers and Participation. *IFLA Journal, 29*, 33–40.

Griffiths, F., Lindenmeyer, A., Powell, J., Lowe, P., & Thorogood, M. (2006). Why are health care interventions delivered over the Internet? A systematic review of the published literature. *Journal of Medical Internet Research, 8*(2), e10.

Gui, M., & Argentin, G. (2011). Digital skills of Internet natives: Different forms of Internet literacy in a random sample of northern Italian high school students. *New Media & Society, 13*(6), 963–980.

Gwizdka, J., & Spence, I. (2007). Implicit measures of lostness and success in web navigation. *Interacting with Computers, 19*(3), 357–369.

Hargittai, E. (2002). Second-level digital divide: Differences in people's online skills. *First Monday, 7*(4). Retrieved March 9, 2014, from http://www.editlib.org/p/95767.

Hargittai, E. (2010). Digital Na(t)ives? Variation in Internet skills and uses among members of the net generation. *Sociological Inquiry, 80*(1), 92–113.

Hargittai, E., & Hinnant, A. (2008). Digital inequality: Differences in young adults' use of the Internet. *Communication Research, 35*(5), 602–621.

Hargittai, E., & Shafer, S. (2006). Differences in actual and perceived online skills: The role of gender. *Social Science Quarterly, 87*(2), 432–448.

Hargittai, E., & Walejko, G. (2008). The participation divide: Content creation and sharing in the digital age. *Information, Communication & Society,* 11(2), 239–256.

Helsper, E. J. (2012). A corresponding fields model of digital inclusion. *Communication Theory, 22*, 403–426.

Helsper, E. J., & Eynon, R. (2010). Digital natives: Where is the evidence? *British Educational Research Journal, 36*(3), 503–520.

Herder, E. (2003). Revisitation patterns and disorientation. Proceedings of the German Workshop on Adaptivity and User Modeling in Interactive Systems, ABIS, 291–294.

Hick, S. (2006). Technology, social inclusion and poverty: An exploratory investigation of a community technology center. *Journal of Technology in Human Services, 24*(1), 53–67.

Hill, J. R. (1999). A conceptual framework for understanding information seeking in open-ended information services. *Educational Technology, Research and Development, 47*(1), 5–27.

Hindman, M. (2009). *The myth of digital democracy.* Princeton: Princeton University Press.

Hoem, J., & Schwebs, T. (2004). Personal publishing and media literacy. Paper presented at the 8th IFIP World Conference on Computers in Education, Cape Town.

Holloway, S. L. G., & Valentine, G. (2003). *Cyberkids—children in the information age.* London: Routledge Falmer.

Hoofnagle, C. J., King, J., Li, S., & Turrow, J. (2010). How different are young adults from older adults when it comes to information privacy attitudes and policies? Retrieved March 24, 2014, from http://ssrn.com/abstract= 1589864.

Hou, H. T., & Wu, S. Y. (2011). Analyzing the social knowledge construction behavioral patterns of an online synchronous collaborative discussion instructional activity using an instant messaging tool: A case study. *Computers & Education, 57*(2), 1459–1468.

Howard, P. N., Rainie, L., & Jones, S. (2001). Days and nights on the Internet: The impact of a diffusing technology. *American Behavioral Scientist, 45*(3), 383–404.

Howe, N., & Strauss, B. (2000). *Millennials rising: The next great generation.* New York, USA: Vintage Books.

Huberman, B., Romero, D. M., & Wu, F. (2009). Social networks that matter: Twitter under the microscope. *First Monday, 14*(1). Retrieved March 24, 2014, from http://firstmonday.org/article/view/2317/2063.

International Telecommunications Union. (2013). World Telecommunication/ICT Indicators database 2013. Retrieved March 24, 2014, from http://www.itu.int.

Ito, M., Horst, H. A., Bittanti, M., Boyd, D. M., Herr-Stephenson, B., Lange, P. G.,. . . Robinson, L. (2008). *Living and learning with new media: Summary of findings from the digital youth project.* Cambridge, MA: The MIT Press.

Ivanitskaya, L., O'Boyle, I., & Casey, A. M. (2006). Health information literacy and competencies of information age students: Results from the Interactive Online Research Readiness Self-Assessment (RRSA). *Journal of Medical Internet Research, 8*(2), e6.

Jaeger, P. T., Bertot, J. C., Thompson, K., Katz, S. M., & Decoster, E. J. (2012). The intersection of public policy and public access: Digital divides, digital literacy, digital inclusion, and public libraries. *Public Library Quarterly, 31*, 1–20.

Jager C. J. & Gillebaard, H. (2010). *Behoeftenonderzoek Mediawijzer.* Dialogic: Utrecht.

Jansen, B. J. (2005). Seeking and implementing automated assistance during the search process. *Information Processing and Management, 41*, 909–928.

Jansen, B. J., & Pooch, U. (2000).Web user studies: A review and framework for future work. *Journal of the American Society of Information Science and Technology, 52*(3), 235–246.

172 • References

Jansen, B. J., & Spink, A. (2003). An analysis of web information seeking and use: Documents retrieved versus documents viewed. Proceedings of the 4th International Conference on Internet Computing, 65–69. Las Vegas, Nevada. June 23–26.

Jenkins, C., Corritore, C. L., & Wiedenbeck, W. (2003). Patterns of information seeking on the Web: A qualitative study of domain expertise and Web expertise. *IT&Society, 1*(3), 64–89.

Jenkins, H. (2006). *Convergence culture: Where old and new media collide.* New York: New York University Press.

Jenkins, H., Purushotma, R., Weigel, M., Clinton, K., & Robinson, A. J. (2009). *Confronting the challenges of participatory culture: Media education for the 21st century.* Cambridge, MA: The MIT Press.

Jones, C., Ramanau, R., Cross, S. J., & Healing, G. (2010). Net generation or digital natives: Is there a distinct new generation entering university? *Computers & Education 54*(3), 722–732.

Jorgenson, B. (2003). Baby boomers, generation X and generation Y: Policy implications for defense forces in the modern era. *Foresight, 5*, 41–49.

Kalmus, V. (2013). Making sense of the social mediation of children's Internet use: Perspectives for interdisciplinary and cross-cultural research. In C. W. Wijnen, S. Trültzsch, & C. Ortner (Eds.), *Medienwelten im Wandel* (pp. 137–149). Wien: Springer.

Katz, I. R. (2007). Testing information literacy in digital environments: ETS's iSkills Assessment. *Information Technology and Libraries, 26*(4), 3–12.

Katz, J. E., & Rice, R. E. (2002). *Social consequences of Internet use: Access, involvement, and interaction.* Cambridge, MA: The MIT Press.

Kennisnet. (2007). *Vier in Balans Monitor, Stand van zaken over ict in het onderwijs.* Kennisnet: Zoetermeer.

Kim, S. (2003). The impact of unequal access to the Internet on earnings: A cross-sectional analysis. *Perspectives on Global Development and Technology, 2*(2), 215–236.

Kim, Y. S., & Merriam, S. B. (2010). Situated learning and identity development in a Korean older adults' computer classroom. *Adult Education Quarterly, 60*(5), 438–455.

Kirschner, P. A., Sweller, J., & Clark, R. E. (2006). Why minimal guidance during instruction does not work: An analysis of the failure of constructivist, discovery, problem-based, experiential, and inquiry-based teaching. *Educational Psychologist, 41*(2), 75–86.

Kling, R. (2000). Learning about information technologies and social change: The contribution of social informatics. *The Information Society, 16*(3), 217–232.

Kolodinsky, J., Cranwell, M., & Rowe, E. (2002). Bridging the generation gap across the digital divide: Teens teaching Internet skills to senior citizens. *Journal of Extension, 40*(3). Retrieved March 24, 2014, from http://www.joe.org/joe/2002june/rb2.php/site_urlindex.php.

Kuhlemeier, H., & Hemker, B. (2007). The impact of computer use at home on students' Internet skills. *Computers & Education, 49*(2), 460–480.

Kuiper, E., Volman, M., & Terwel, J. (2004). Internet als informatiebron in het onderwijs: Een verkenning van de literatuur. *Pedagogische Studiën, 81,* 423–443.

Kuriyan, R., & Toyama, K. (2007). Review of research on rural PC kiosks. Retrieved from http://research.microsoft.com/research/tem/kiosks.

Kwan, M. P. (2001). Cyberspatial cognition and individual access to information: The behavioral foundation of cybergeography. *Environment and Planning B: Planning and Design, 28,* 21–37.

Land, S. M., & Greene, B. A. (2000). Project-based learning with the World Wide Web: A qualitative study of resource integration. *Educational Technology, Research and Development, 48*(1), 45–68.

Lankshear, C., & Knobel, M. (2011). New literacies: Everyday practices and classroom learning. 3rd ed. Maidenhead and New York: Open University Press.

Larsson, L. (2002). Digital literacy checklist. Retrieved from http://depts.washington.edu/hserv/teaching/diglit.

Lawton, C. A. (1994). Gender differences in way-finding strategies: Relationship to spatial ability and spatial anxiety. *Sex Roles, 30,* 765–779.

Lee, M. J. (2005). Expanding hypertext: Does it address disorientation? *Journal of Computer-Mediated Communication, 10*(3), article 6.

Lenhart, A. (2009). *Adults and social network websites.* Washington, DC: Pew Internet & American Life Project.

Lenhart, A., Madden, M., & Hitlin, P. (2005). *Teens and technology.* Washington, DC: Pew Internet & American Life Project.

Lenhart, A., Purcell, K., Smith, A., & Zickuhr, K. (2010). *Social media & mobile Internet use among teens and young adults.* Washington, DC: Pew Internet & American Life Project.

Leu, D. J., Zawilinski, L., Castek, J., Banerjee, M., Housand, B., Liu, Y., & O'Neil, M. (2007).What is new about the new literacies of online reading comprehension? In L. Rush, J. Eakle, & A. Berger (Eds.), *Secondary school literacy: What research reveals for classroom practices* (pp. 37–68). Urbana, IL: National Council of Teachers of English.

Levin, D., & Arafeh, S. (2002). *The Digital Disconnect: The Widening gap between Internet-savy students and their schools.* Washington, DC: Pew Internet and American Life Project.

Litt, E. (2012). Measuring users' Internet skills: A review of past assessments and a look towards the future. *New media and society, 15*(4), 612–630.

Livingstone, S. (2003). The changing nature and uses of media literacy. Retrieved from http://www.lse.ac.uk/collections/media@lse/.

Livingstone, S. (2008). Taking risky opportunities in youthful content creation: Teenagers' use of social networking sites for intimacy, privacy and self-expression. *New Media & Society, 10*(3), 393–411.

Livingstone, S., & Helsper, E. (2007). Gradations in digital inclusion: Children, young people and the digital divide. *New media & society, 9*(4), 671–696.

Livingstone, S., Van Couvering, E., & Thumim, N. (2005). Adult media literacy: A review of the research literature. London: Office of Communications.

Long, S. (2006). Exploring the wiki world: The new face of collaboration. *New Library World, 107*(3–4), 157–159.

Lorenzen, M. (2002). The land of confusion? High school students and their use of the world wide web for research. *Research Strategies, 18*(2), 151–163.

Madden, M. (2003). *America's online pursuits.* Washington, DC: Pew Internet and American Life Project.

Mansell, R. (2002). From digital divides to digital entitlements in knowledge societies. *Current Sociology, 50*(3), 407–426.

Marchionini, G. (1995). *Information seeking in electronic environments.* New York: Cambridge University Press.

Markey, K. (2007). Twenty-five years of end-user searching, Part 1: Research findings. *Journal of the American Society for Information Science and Technology, 58*(8), 1071–1081.

Martin, A. (2006). *A framework for digital literacy.* Glasgow: University of Glasgow.

Mayer, R. (2004). Should there be a three-strikes rule against pure discovery learning? The case for guided methods of instruction. *American Psychologist, 59*(1), 14–19.

McDonald, S., & Stevenson, R. J. (1998). Effects of text structure and prior knowledge of the learner on navigation in hypertext. *Human Factors, 40*(1), 18–27.

McGonigal, J. (2008). Why I love bees: A case study in collective intelligence gaming. In K. Saln (Ed.), *The ecology of games: Connecting youth, games, and learning* (pp. 199–228). Cambridge, MA: The MIT Press.

Miller, K. (2006). *Organizational communication, Approaches and processes.* Belmont, CA: Thomson Wadsworth.

Mizrach, S. (1998). *From orality to teleliteracy.* Retrieved from http:www.fiu.edu/-mizrachs/orality.htm.

Mossberger, K., Tolbert, C. J., & Hamilton, A. (2012). Measuring digital citizenship: Mobile access and broadband. *International Journal of Communication, 6,* 2492–2528.

Mossberger, K., Johns, K., & King, B. (2006). *The digital divide and economic opportunity: Does Internet use matter for less-skilled workers.* Retrieved from http://www.uic.edu/orgs/stresearch/Documents/.

Mossberger, K., Tolbert, C. J., & Stansbury, M. (2003). Virtual inequality: Beyond the digital divide. Washington, DC: Georgetown University Press.

Müller, H., Gove, J. L., & Webb, J. S. (2012). Understanding tablet use: A multimethod exploration. Paper presented at the Mobile HCI Conference 2012, September 21–24 in San Francisco CA, USA.

Murphy, E., Kuber, R., McAllister, G., & Strain, P. (2008). An empirical investigation into the difficulties experienced by visually impaired Internet users. *Universal Access to the Information Society, 7,* 79–91.

Nahuis, R., & De Groot, H. L. F. (2003). Rising skill premia: You ain't see nothing yet. *Tjalling C. Koopmans Institute Discussion Paper Series, 3*(2), 1–50.

Newhagen, J. E., & Bucy, E. P. (2004). Routes to media access. In E. P. Bucy & J. E. Newhagen (Eds.), *Media access: Social and psychological dimensions of new technology use* (pp. 3–23). London: Psychology Press.

Nic, H. (2009). Improving computer interaction for older adults. *ACM SIGACCESS Accessibility and Computing, 93*, 11–17.

Nielsen, J. (2002). *Usability for senior citizens*. Retrieved from http://www.useit.com/alertbox/20020428.html.

Oblinger, D. (2003). Boomers, gen-xers, millenials: Understanding the new students. *Educause Review, 38*(4), 37–47.

O'Hara, K. (2004). Curb cuts on the information highway: Older adults and the Internet. *Technical Communication Quarterly, 13*(4), 423–445.

Ono, H., & Zavodny, M. (2003). Gender and the Internet. *Social Science Quarterly, 84*(1), 111–121.

Pandolfini, C., Impicciatore, P., & Bonati, M. (2000). Parents on the Web: Risks for quality management of cough in children. *Pediatrics, 105*, A1–A8.

Papert, S. (1996). *The connected family: Bridging the digital generation gap*. Atlanta, GA: Longstreet.

Pearce, K. E., & Rice, R. E. (2013). Digital divides from access to activities: Comparing mobile and personal computer Internet users. *Journal of Communication, 63*(4), 721–744.

Peluchette, J., & Karl, K. (2010). Examining students' intended image on Facebook: What were they thinking?! *Journal of Education for Business, 85*, 30–37.

Pew Internet and American Life Project. (2012). Online survey data set. Retrieved March 24, 2014, from http://www.pewinternet.org/.

Potosky, D. (2007). The Internet knowledge (iKnow) measure. *Computers in Human Behavior, 23*(6), 337–348.

Powell, T. A. (2000). *Web design: The complete reference*. Berkeley, CA: McGraw-Hill Osborne Media.

Prensky, M. (2001). Digital natives, digital immigrants. *On the Horizon: NCB University Press, 9*(5), 1–10.

Prensky, M. (2005a). Engage me or enrage me: What today's learners demand. *Educause Review, 40*(5), 61–65.

Prensky, M. (2005b). Listen to the natives. *Educational Leadership, 63*(4), 8–13.

Quan-Haase, A., Wellman, B., Witte, J., & Hampton, K. N. (2002). Capitalizing on the Internet: Network capital, participatory capital, and sense of community. In B. Wellman & C. Haythornthwaite (Eds.), *The Internet in everyday life* (pp. 291–324). Oxford: Blackwell.

Rangaswami, N. (2008). Telecenters and Internet cafés: The case of ICTs in small businesses. *Asian Journal of Communication, 18*(4), 365–378.

Redecker, C., Haché, A., & Centeno, C. (2010). *Using information and communication technologies to promote education and employment opportunities for immigrants and ethnic minorities*. Seville: JRC(European Commission)/IPTS.

Reeves, B., & Nass, C. (1996). *The media equation: How people treat computers, television, and new media like real people and places*. New York, NY: Cambridge University press.

Rheingold, H. (2012). *Net Smart: How to thrive online*. Cambridge, MA: MIT Press Books.

Rogers, W., & Fisk, A.D. (2000). Human factors, applied cognition, and aging. In F. I. M. Craik (Ed.), *The handbook of aging and cognition*, 2nd ed. Mahwah, NJ: Lawrence Erlbaum Associates.

Rubin, J. (1994). *Handbook of usability testing: How to plan, design, and conduct effective tests.* New York: John Wiley & Sons.

Rury, J. L. (2005). *Education and social change: Themes in the history of American schooling.* Mahwah, NJ: Lawrence Erlbaum Associates.

Salomon, G. (1977). Effects of encouraging Israeli mothers to co-observe sesame street with their five-year-olds. *Child Development, 48*(3), 1146–1151.

Scheufele, D. A., & Nisbet, M. C. (2002). Being a citizen online—New opportunities and dead ends, SUM. *Harvard International Journal of Press-Politics, 7*(3), 55–75.

Schradie, J. (2011). The digital production gap: The digital divide and Web 2.0 collide. *Poetics, 34*(4–5), 221–235.

Scott, T. J., & O'Sullivan, M. K. (2005). Analyzing student search strategies: Making a case for integrating information literacy skills into the curriculum. *Teacher Librarian, 33*(1), 21–25.

Selwyn, N. (2003). Apart from technology: Understanding people's non-use of information and communication technologies in everyday life. *Technology in Society, 25*, 99–116.

Selwyn, N. (2005). The social processes of learning to use computers. *Social Science Computer Review, 23*, 122–135.

Selwyn, N. (2013). Education in a digital world, global perspectives on technology and education. New York and London: Routledge.

Selwyn, N., Gorard, S., & Furlong, J. (2006). *Adult learning in the digital age: Information technology and the learning society.* London and New York: Routledge.

Servon, L. J., & Nelson, M. K. (2001). Community technology centers: Narrowing the digital divide in low-income communities. *Journal of Urban Affairs, 23*(3–4), 279–290.

Shepperd, S., Charnock, D., & Gann, B. (1999). Helping patients access high quality health information. *British Medical Journal, 319*(7212), 764–766.

Shirky, C. (2003). *Power laws, weblogs, and inequality.* Retrieved from http://www.shirky.com/writings/powerlaw_weblog.html.

Siegfried, S., Bates, M. J., & Wilde, D. N. (1993). A profile of end-user searching behavior by humanities scholars: The Getty Online Searching Project Report No. 2. *Journal of the American Society for Information Science, 44*, 273–291.

Sifry, D. (2005). *State of the Blogosphere March 2005, part 3: The A-list and the long tail.* Retrieved March 24, 2014, from http://www.sifry.com/alerts/archives/000301.html.

Sigurbjörnsson, B., & Van Zwol, R. (2008). Flickr tag recommendation based on collective knowledge. WWW'08: Proc. the 17th international conference on World Wide Web, Beijing, China, 327–336.

Søby, M. (2003). *Digital competences: From ICT skills to digital bildung.* Oslo: University of Oslo.

Somekh, B., Lewin, C., Mavers, D., Harrison, C., Haw, K., Fisher, T., ... Scrimshaw, P. (2002). *ImpaCT2: Pupils' and teachers' perceptions of ICT in the home, school and community.* Annersley, UK: British Educational Communications and Technology Agency.

Spink, A., Wolfram, D., Jansen, B. J., & Saracevic, T. (2001). Searching the web: The public and their queries. *Journal of the American Society for Information Science, 53,* 226–234.

Stone, L. (1969). Literacy and education in England 1640–1900. *Past & Present, 42,* 69–139.

Talja, S. (2005). The social and discursive construction of computing skills. *Journal of the American Society for Information Science and Technology, 56*(1), 13–22.

Tapscott, D. (1998). *Growing up digital: The rise of the Net generation.* London: McGraw-Hill.

Tarasewich, P. (2003). Designing mobile commerce applications. *Communications of the ACM, 46*(12), 57–60.

Thatcher, A. (2008). Web search strategies: The influence of Web experience and task type. *Information Processing and Management, 44*(3), 1308–1313.

Tichenor, P. J., Donohue, G. A., & Olien, C. N. (1970). Mass media flow and differential growth in knowledge. *Public Opinion Quarterly, 34*(2), 159–170.

Tilly, C. (1998). *Durable inequality.* Berkeley, CA: University of California Press.

Tyner, K. (1998). *Literacy in a Digital World.* Mahwah NJ: Lawrence Erlbaum Associates.

UNDP. (2009). *Human development report 2009. Overcoming barriers: Human mobility and development.* New York: Human Development Report Office.

Valkenburg, P. M., & Peter, J. (2007). Preadolescents' and adolescents' online communication and their closeness to friends. *Developmental Psychology, 43*(2), 267–277.

Valkenburg, P. M., Peter, J., & Schouten, A. P. (2006). Friend networking sites and their relationship to adolescents' well-being and social self-esteem. *CyberPsychology & Behavior, 9*(5), 584–590.

Van der Geest, T., Van der Meij, H., & Van Puffelen, C. (2014). Self-assessed and actual Internet skills of people with visual impairments. Universal Access in the Information Society, 13, 161–174.

Van Deursen, A. J. A. M. (2010). *Internet skills, vital assets in an information society.* Enschede: Univeristy of Twente.

Van Deursen, A. J. A. M. (2012). Internet skill-related problems in accessing online health information and services. *International Journal of Medical Informatics, 81*(1), 61–72.

Van Deursen, A. J. A. M., & Pieterson, W. (2006). The Internet as a service channel in the Public Sector. A substitute or complement of traditional service channels? Paper presented at the 58th Annual Conference of the International Communication Association, Dresden.

Van Deursen, A. J. A. M., & Van Diepen, S. (2013). Information and strategic Internet skills of secondary students: A performance test. *Computers & Education, 63,* 218–226.

Van Deursen, A. J. A. M., & Van Dijk, J. A. G. M. (2009a). Improving digital skills for the use of online public information and services. *Government Information Quarterly, 26,* 333–340.

Van Deursen, A. J. A. M., & Van Dijk, J. A. G. M. (2009b). Using the Internet: Skill related problems in users' online behavior. *Interacting with Computers, 21,* 393–402.

Van Deursen, A. J. A. M., & Van Dijk, J. A. G. M. (2010). Measuring Internet skills. *International Journal of Human-Computer Interaction, 26*(10), 891–916.

Van Deursen, A. J. A. M., & Van Dijk, J. A. G. M. (2011a). Internet skills and the digital divide. *New Media & Society, 13*(6), 893–911.

Van Deursen, A. J. A. M., & Van Dijk, J. A. G. M. (2011b). Internet skills performance tests: Are people ready for eHealth? *Journal of Medical Internet Research, 13*(2), e35.

Van Deursen, A. J. A. M., & Van Dijk, J. A. G. M. (2014a). The digital divide shifts to differences in usage. *New Media & Society, 16(3),* 507–526.

Van Deursen, A. J. A. M., & Van Dijk, J. A. G. M. (2014b). Loss of labor time due to skill insufficiencies and malfunctioning ICT. *International Journal of Manpower, 35*(5), in press.

Van Deursen, A. J. A. M., Courtois, C., & Van Dijk, J. A. G. M. (2014). Internet skills, sources of support and benefiting from Internet use. *International Journal of Human-Computer Interaction, 30*(4), 278–290.

Van Deursen, A. J. A. M., Van Dijk, J. A. G. M., & Ebbers, W. (2006). Why e-government usage lags behind: Explaining the gap between potential and actual usage of electronic public services in the Netherlands. *Lecture Notes in Computer Science, 4084,* 269–280.

Van Deursen, A. J. A. M., Van Dijk, J. A. G. M., & Peters, O. (2011). Rethinking Internet skills. The contribution of gender, age, education, internet experience, and hours online to medium- and content-related Internet skills. *Poetics, 39,* 125–144.

Van Deursen, A. J. A. M., Van Dijk, J. A. G. M., Peters, O. (2012). Proposing a survey instrument for measuring operational, formal, information and strategic Internet skills. *International Journal of Human-Computer Interaction, 28*(12), 827–837.

Van Dijk, J. A. G. M. (1999). *The network society: Social aspects of new media.* London: Sage.

Van Dijk, J. A. G. M. (2005). *The deepening divide: Inequality in the information society.* London: Sage.

Van Dijk, J. A. G. M. (2006). Digital divide research, achievements and shortcomings. *Poetics, 34*(4–5), 221–235.

Van Dijk, J. A. G. M. (2012). *The network society* (3rd edition). London: Sage.

Van Dijk, J. A. G. M., & Hacker, K. (2003). The digital divide as a complex and dynamic phenomenon. *The Information Society, 19*(4), 315–327.

Van Dijk, J. A. G. M., De Haan, J., & Rijken, S. (2000). *Digitalisering van de Leefwereld, een onderzoek naar informatie en communicatietechnologie en sociale ongelijkheid.* The Hague: SCP.

Wallace, R., Kupperman, J., Krajcik, J., & Soloway, E. (2000). Science on the Web: Students online in a sixth-grade classroom. *Journal of the Learning Sciences, 9*(1), 75–104.

Walraven, A., Brand-Gruwel, S., & Boshuizen, H. P. A. (2008). Information-problem solving: A review of problems students encounter and instructional solutions. *Computers in Human Behavior, 24*(3), 623–648.

Wandke, H., Sengpiel, M., & Sönksen, M. (2012). Myths about older people's use of information and communication technology. *Gerontology, 58*(6), 564–570.

Warschauer, M. (2003). *Technology and social inclusion: Rethinking the digital divide.* Cambridge, MA: The MIT Press.

Warschauer, M., & Ames, M. (2010). Can one laptop per child save the world's poor? *Journal of International Affairs, 64*(1), 33–51.

Wasserman, I. M., & Richmond-Abbott, M. (2005). Gender and the Internet: Causes of variation in access, level, and scope of use. *Social Science Quarterly, 86*(1), 252–270.

Webster, J., & Ahuja, J. S. (2006). Enhancing the design of web navigation systems: The influence of user disorientation on engagement and performance. *Management Information Systems Quarterly, 30*(3), 661–678.

Wellman, B., & Haythornthwaite, C. (2002). *The Internet in everyday life.* Oxford: Blackwell.

Witte, J. C., & Mannon, S. E. (2010). *The Internet and social inequalities.* New York, London: Routledge.

Xie, B. (2003). Older adults, computers, and the Internet: Future directions. *Gerontechnology, 2*(4), 289–305.

Yu, L. (2010). How poor informationally are the information poor?: Evidence from an empirical study of daily and regular information Practices of individuals. *Journal of Documentation, 66*(6), 906–933.

Zauberman, G. (2003). The intertemporal dynamics of consumer lock-in. *Journal of Consumer Research, 30*(3), 405–419.

Zillien, N., & Hargittai, E. (2009). Digital distinction: Status-specific types of Internet usage. *Social Science Quarterly, 90*(2), 274–291.

Index

Page numbers and page ranges in bold indicate figures, tables, and subheadings.